Published in 2009 by Age Concern Books

1268 London Road, London SW16 4ER, United Kingdom

ISBN: 978 0 86242 443 5

A catalogue record for this book is available from the British Library.

The four national Age Concerns in the UK have joined together with Help the Aged to form new national charities dedicated to improving the lives of older people.

Edited by: Pamela Skipwith

Cover design by: Vincent McEvoy

Designed and typeset by: Design and Media Solutions, Maidstone

Printed and bound in Great Britain by: Bell & Bain Ltd, Glasgow

Mixed Sources

Product group from well-managed forests and other controlled sources

www.fsc.org   Cert no. TT-COC-002769
© 1996 Forest Stewardship Council

FSC

Contents

Introduction

Why manage your money online?

There is a whole host of reasons why it could make sense for you to manage your money online.

To begin with, it could give you access to a range of products and services that are only available via the internet, from web savings accounts to online gas and electricity tariffs and special deals on insurance. Some companies only operate through the internet; other businesses may have a physical presence on the high street or operate over the telephone but also offer additional deals to customers who are prepared to run their account via their computer.

And it is not just a question of choice. Firms that offer some or all of their products over the internet can cut their own costs by, for example, not having a network of offices, or by not letting you access your money in a branch. Those savings can enable them to offer you more competitive deals, thus saving you money.

There is another benefit. One of the internet's most useful functions is the way it lets you easily and quickly compare dozens, hundreds or even thousands of different products at the same time.

With the click of a mouse you can identify the best deal for your circumstances and, hopefully, avoid the expensive, the second-rate or the just plain wrong.

It is also possible to deal with many government departments and other official bodies through the internet. From filing your tax return to requesting a pension forecast to finding out whether you qualify for extra help with your council tax; again, this is all possible from the comfort of your own home and at a time that suits you.

And of course learning to manage your money online could be just the start. A computer that is connected to the internet offers endless opportunities; emailing friends and family, making free or cheap calls through computer telephony, planning and booking holidays, finding details of local evening classes, checking the weather, locating tradespeople, renewing your road tax, researching your family tree, making contact with people who share similar interests through internet message boards and chat rooms, downloading music, listening to the radio, watching television and films, and so on. The possibilities are endless.

Who is this book for?

This book is for people who want to run their finances online but aren't sure where to start. It doesn't assume any prior knowledge of using a computer (and includes a glossary of useful terms at the end) although it should still be useful even if you have used one before.

It will take you through the practical steps of choosing, setting up and managing a variety of accounts online. It will also offer advice about how to do this safely by protecting your personal and financial information at every stage.

One thing this book is *not* is a detailed technical guide to choosing and buying a computer. It will touch on some of the relevant issues, and offer some pointers, but it may be prudent to seek additional professional advice to ensure you buy the right computer for your needs.

It will also be possible to use this book even if you don't have – or plan to get – your own computer.

By the end, I hope you will feel confident about your ability to manage as much of your world online as you wish and ready to take the plunge.

Let's dive in.

1

How to get online

The easiest and safest place to manage your money on the internet is on your own computer in the privacy of your own home. It means you can go online whenever you wish and, by controlling who has access to the machine, you can help keep your personal data secure. We'll talk more about being safe online in the next chapter.

Choosing a computer

This can seem very daunting but the good news is that computers are generally faster, more powerful, more reliable and, in many cases, cheaper than they've ever been.

Happily, as home computers become increasingly popular, there is no shortage of information. Ask friends and family, look online if you can get access to the internet (most local libraries offer free web access – see the end of this chapter for more on this), consult magazines and newspapers. Age Concern has several books available that you may find useful to help those new to computing, in particular *Computing for Beginners* (see back of book for details of how to order).

You may have a specialist computer shop near you where you can discuss your needs in detail. The scope for independent advice may be more limited in the major high street electrical retailers, but staff should still be able to answer your queries satisfactorily. If they can't, consider going elsewhere. Buying a computer is an important – and expensive – purchase, and it's important to buy from someone you trust who is knowledgeable in this area.

I said in the introduction that this book would not offer in-depth technical advice about choosing a computer. It is a very personal decision and depends largely on your own requirements and budget.

However, I will run through some of the areas you need to consider. The key is to work out what you think you would like it to do and then try to identify the best option for your circumstances.

There is no point paying for a top-of-the-range or extremely powerful machine if it is stuffed full of features that you will never use. Equally, given the rapid increase in computer technology, it is wise to avoid buying the cheapest or most basic model because of the risk of it becoming obsolete too quickly.

Another important decision is whether you want a laptop so you can use the computer in different rooms in your house – or indeed when you are out and about or on holiday. Or would you prefer a desktop machine that can live permanently in your study or living room?

To PC or not to PC

The second choice is between the two main types of computer: a PC or a Mac.

The vast majority of home computers are PCs, which run a version of Microsoft Windows operating software, the latest version of which is called Vista (although other operating systems are available).

Macs have a different operating system (although they can now run Microsoft software) and are beloved by aficionados because of their attractive design. They are considered excellent for projects involving lots of graphics or music/video editing. Most Mac software is designed by Apple, the company that makes the machines, meaning different programmes work together very smoothly. Macs are also widely considered to be less vulnerable (but not immune) to computer viruses.

However, beware. Although Macs and PCs are now more compatible than they have ever been, you cannot share software between them, and not all websites can be fully accessed by the programmes that Macs use to browse the internet. The cheapest Mac is also much more expensive than the cheapest PC, although it is not really a fair comparison since a basic Mac will tend to be a much more powerful machine than an entry level PC.

The choice largely comes down to your personal preference, so the sensible decision is to have a look at both and see which appeals more. It is also worth considering which type of computer your friends and family have. If the people you are likely to call on for help and advice are all PC users, it might make sense to follow in their footsteps.

Shopping list

The next stage is to consider how much power/memory you want, and what software and other pieces of computer hardware you might also need. Most PCs and Macs are sold as packages, which 'bundle' together various bits of hardware (the physical parts of your computer) and software (the programmes that run on your computer) and they should come with everything you need for the computer to work and connect to the internet.

You may decide to buy one of these straight off the shelf. Alternatively, you may wish to pay more to upgrade individual components to a higher specification, or save some money by removing items you do not want.

If you do decide you would like a more tailored computer, you may wish to consider the following:

• What kind of **CPU** (central processing unit) or processor does the machine have? The speed of your processor determines how fast your computer can process data and is usually measured in megahertz (MHz), or gigahertz (GHz). Two of the most popular PC processors are Intel's Pentium and AMD's Athlon. Unless you plan to do some very complicated stuff on your computer, the standard CPU you are offered will probably suffice, but it is worth making sure it is relatively new and relatively powerful, or at least not a very outdated model.

- How much **memory** or storage capacity does the computer have? Even fairly basic computers now often come with a **hard drive** of 160GB or 250GB, which will be perfectly adequate for most people when coupled with RAM (random access memory) of 1GB or above.
- Unless you want to do fancy things with graphics and sound, the standard graphics and sound cards should be fine.
- You may wish to pay more for a larger monitor, or upgrade to a wireless keyboard and mouse. You may find a printer is included or available with your computer bundle.
- Most modern computers will come with a **modem**, the machine your computer needs to connect to the internet. If not, it is often supplied by your **ISP** or internet service provider (see below).
- What **software** comes with the machine? It is often cheaper to buy software as part of the 'bundle' – but make sure you are not paying extra for software you will never use.
- What sort of technical support is on offer? How long is support offered? When is it available? What does it cost? Many technical support helplines use premium-rate telephone numbers.
- Be very wary of paying for an extended warranty. Many high street retailers make more profit on selling insurance policies than computers. If you are tempted, check exactly what is covered – your household insurance may already protect you.

Choosing an internet service provider and email account

Next you need to select an Internet Service Provider (or ISP), the company that will manage your internet connection and provide you with an email account (or accounts).

You will need to provide an email address when you register for any online account (or for online access to an existing account) as this will be the company's primary means of communication with you. In some cases your email address will itself be part of the information you need to provide when you access your accounts.

If you wish, you can set up multiple email accounts but make sure you know which account is registered with each provider.

 When you buy a computer, you sometimes get a free trial subscription with a particular ISP. You do not have to activate this but it may be useful to use in the short term to get you online so you can shop around to compare your options. Popular ISPs include AOL, BT.com, Virgin, Tiscali, and TalkTalk.

Your email address is usually: *thenameyouchoose@thenameoftheISP.co.uk* (or *.com*). Some ISPs will let you have multiple email addresses through one account.

Choose your email address carefully; common names are unlikely to be available, although you can often find something near, such as *johnsmith999@...* You can also try reversing your name, or swapping the first letters of your first and last name so that Sarah Hughes becomes *hughessarah@...* or *harahsughes@...*

Most email addresses are not case sensitive. Don't include the year you were born as it makes it easy to guess your complete date of birth, which is often a piece of information used to help identify yourself online.

There are essentially two types of connection: **dial-up**, which uses your existing telephone line to connect to the internet (and means you cannot make or receive phone calls while you are on the internet); and **broadband**, which works differently and does not tie up your telephone line. Broadband connections are 'always on', meaning you are permanently connected to the internet, and let you download material from the internet much more quickly than older 'narrow band' connections. Your connection speed will partly depend on whereabouts in the country you live and how much you are prepared to pay, but broadband is usually defined as having a minimum connection speed of 512Kbps, which is roughly ten times as fast as a standard telephone dial-up connection.

The bill for using dial-up connections usually depends on the amount of time you spend on the internet. Broadband deals tend to charge you according to the amount of information or data that you transfer between your computer and the internet, and the speed of your connection. The amount of data will vary depending on what you do on the internet. Downloading lots of music or regularly watching video content online would involve the transfer of much more data than just reading text or accessing savings accounts online.

Make sure you understand the *pricing structure* of any deal you sign up to. It may be cheaper to arrange your internet connection via your own or a rival telephone provider such as BT or Virgin. Beware of very cheap offers: some companies may compromise on customer service, for example, using expensive premium-rate telephone numbers.

Also, *check the small print* of your contract. Are you signing up for a certain period of time? If you are being offered reduced payments as an introductory offer, what will the full price be? How can you cancel?

*If you travel regularly, you may wish to choose an ISP that will let you check your email via the internet from any computer (**webmail**), as well as via the software installed onto your own machine.*

Your ISP will be able to advise you about the equipment and software you require and should provide it as part of the deal when you sign up.

For more information about broadband, visit: *www.direct.gov.uk/en/HomeAndCommunity/ TechnologyInYourHome/index.htm*.

For more information about broadband availability in your area, visit: *www.samknows.com/ broadband/*.

The public route

If you don't want or can't afford to buy your own computer, it is still possible to get online using public facilities, often at small or no cost.

A government-sponsored organisation called UK Online offers free internet access at a variety of centres on the high street; in libraries, internet cafes and community centres across the UK. Find your nearest centre at: *www.ukonlinecentres.com/ consumer/* or phone 0800 771234. For Scotland, which has different funding, phone 0808 100 1091.

Some learndirect centres across England, Wales and Northern Ireland also offer free internet access. Find your nearest centre at: *www.learndirect-skills.co.uk/centres/* or phone 0800 101901.

For information about free internet access in libraries in Northern Ireland, visit: *www.ni-libraries.net/, Scotland*: *www.slainte.org.uk/* and Wales: *www.library.wales.org/*.

There are also commercial internet cafes (sometimes called 'cyber cafes') across the whole of the UK, which generally charge by the hour. Look in your local *Yellow Pages* or telephone directory for details of those near you.

However, there are some things you need to consider when you are using a machine that does not belong to you.

From a practical point of view, you will only have access to the computer – and therefore the internet – between certain hours, and not necessarily at a time that suits you. The length of sessions may be restricted, especially during busy periods, and there may be very limited access on bank holidays or at times like Easter or Christmas.

The other issue is security. Remember, these machines are in a public place and will be used by other people. You will be visible to those around you, as will the sites you visit.

You should, therefore, be sensible about protecting any confidential paperwork you need to have with you in order, for instance, to manage your bank account.

Similarly, there are various practical steps you can take to safeguard your confidential information when using a public machine:

- Think carefully before using an unfamiliar machine to access or input confidential information. Be guided by your instincts – if you feel uncomfortable, stop.
- Never leave the machine unattended while you are using it, especially if you have signed in (or 'logged in') to an account.
- Never save any information to the computer's local hard drive as this could be accessed by anyone else who uses the machine.
- Always sign out (or 'log out') of any sites you have visited; don't just close the window as that may not shut down your connection.
- Always delete the computer's own record of which sites you have visited.
- Always delete 'cookies' – the small files that websites store on your hard drive so they can recognise you and remember your settings or

preferences when you visit them again.

- Always refuse any request to 'remember' your password or other details because this could potentially allow someone else to access your confidential information.
- Don't forget to collect anything you have sent to the printer.

We'll look at protecting yourself online in more detail in the next chapter.

Summary

Choosing a computer and getting yourself onto the internet may seem daunting, but the truth is, it has never been easier, quicker or cheaper to arrange.

It's possible to walk into a high street electrical store today and emerge minutes later with an extremely powerful machine that can easily cope with what most of us would want to do. With a little bit of research you should find the perfect machine for your needs.

If you feel nervous, ask friends and family if you can have a go on their computer before you commit yourself to buying your own. Alternatively, take advantage of the facilities in your local library or internet cafe, remembering to use your common sense about protecting sensitive personal information.

Once you have a computer, getting yourself onto the internet should also be straightforward. Remember there are many sources of free advice available, so if in doubt, ask!

2

How to be safe online

The first step towards being safe online is to understand the dangers.

Just connecting to the internet exposes your machine to a range of nasty programmes that can sabotage or destroy your computer. Similarly, your personal details can also become vulnerable, leaving you at risk of fraud or even identity theft.

The threat is real but don't panic; you can protect yourself by taking some simple steps and, as long as you remain vigilant and use your common sense, you should be able to use the internet with confidence. Macs are generally considered less susceptible to attack than PCs but are not invincible.

This chapter will cover two main areas: how to protect against the physical risks to your computer, and how to safeguard yourself against the less tangible but equally dangerous threat to your personal information.

Your computer: the physical threat

On the basis that forewarned is forearmed, here are some of the main hazards, plus guidance about how to counter them.

Viruses are malicious programmes designed by hackers to replicate themselves and spread from one computer to another, causing enormous damage. They can destroy your operating system, scramble files saved to your hard drive, stop applications working or even switch off your security software, leaving you vulnerable to further attack. Many viruses are transmitted via email attachments. Some – known as **trojans** – are disguised as something else, such as a game or screensaver programme. Viruses can also be passed on by certain websites – either when you download a piece of software or sometimes just by going to the site itself. Another type of virus known as a 'worm' spreads over the internet from one machine to another. Once infected, a computer will search the web to find other vulnerable machines and then send them a copy of the worm, which in turn looks for other recipients.

Another type of malevolent software (**malware**) is called 'spyware'. Unlike a virus, its aim is not to replicate itself but to bury itself in your computer's hard drive from where it can cause all sorts of mischief, including running unwelcome adverts, downloading other viruses, hijacking the browser programme you use to access the internet and scanning your files for private information, such as passwords or credit card numbers, which it then tries to send back to its originator. Once it's established, malware can be very difficult to remove.

Spam refers to unsolicited commercial emails sent out in bulk mailings. Spam emails are usually adverts, such as those for fake pharmaceutical products, or invitations to view pornographic or gambling websites. Some spam emails even promise to block your account from further spam but, in fact, the very act of responding verifies that your email address is active, making you the target for even more mail.

Spam is also one of the main routes for the transmission of viruses. In fact, it is thought to constitute the vast majority of all email traffic, meaning it hampers the collective capacity and speed of the internet for us all, as well as clogging up the inboxes of millions of individuals. It can be very time-consuming to delete such emails manually, many of which contain highly offensive images and language.

Some spam represents a more insidious threat. So-called **phishing** emails purport to come from your bank or other financial provider. The emails – which often appear highly official and use real logos and branding – invite you to 'confirm' your details but actually direct you to fake websites where fraudsters hope to capture your confidential personal information.

The fight back

The good news is that there are a number of steps you can take to protect your machine. Your computer's own operating system or your ISP may provide some defence but you should not rely solely on either.

The most obvious starting point is to install **anti-virus software**. This monitors all incoming emails and attachments to check for viruses or other malware. It also examines files you open or data you download to check for infection. Additionally, it regularly scans your entire computer to ensure there are no nasty surprises lurking anywhere.

There is a huge range of anti-virus software available. Reputable providers include Symantec, McAfee and Kaspersky. Your computer may come with pre-installed anti-virus software or a trial subscription. You can also download free basic versions from the web – although you should be extremely careful before installing software from an unfamiliar site because such a programme could itself be malware.

However, to be truly effective against constantly emerging and mutating threats, your software must have an automatic update facility – and be left switched on at all times – so you may wish to consider buying a full subscription to a well-known programme.

A number of companies offer free web-based detection programmes that will inspect a machine for viruses or other malicious software. You may wish to run such a programme before using an unfamiliar machine for the first time. Sites offering this service include *www.antispyware.com*, *www.webroot.com/uk*

and *www.stopzilla.com*. You should of course only download software from reputable sites.

Many anti-virus programmes also include a **firewall**, which acts as a barrier between your private computer and the public internet. It checks all data being transferred between the two against certain criteria before allowing it through. Your computer's operating system (such as Windows Vista or Mac OS X) may contain a basic firewall although, again, you should consider upgrading to a more sophisticated version and you should never turn it off.

It is also important to ensure you run the latest version of your operating system and other applications because these are generally more secure than their predecessors. Microsoft and Apple both regularly update their operating systems and other software to take account of new threats. Existing customers can download something called a 'patch' from the company website, which will amend the old version stored on their computer. Patches often also fix problems or 'bugs' in earlier versions of software or add extra features. Both Microsoft and Apple's operating systems can be set to search for updates automatically; it is also a good idea to check periodically yourself. For more information, go to *www.update.microsoft.com/* or *www.apple.com/softwareupdate/* or indeed the website of the maker of any other software installed on your machine.

Whichever browser programme you use to go online (i.e. Internet Explorer, Firefox or Safari) make sure you take full advantage of its **safety** settings. All browsers offer various means by which to control exposure to the internet, usually via the Tools or Options menu. You can use parental controls to limit access to certain sites, to prevent file downloads or block specific programmes. You can also block 'pop-up' adverts, which can contain viruses.

Make sure any site is secure before entering confidential information. Many sites use something called the SSL protocol to guarantee your data is safe. Look out for the letters **https** in front of the web address, and a small padlock somewhere in the address bar. Clicking on the padlock brings up details of the site's 'digital certificate', which is issued by an independent third party and authenticates the site's security standards. Reputable sites should also have a privacy policy detailing what personal information the company retains (and for how long) and any third parties with whom they share it. If in doubt, check. If the organisation is not happy to tell you – or indeed you cannot make contact with them – then that is itself a compelling reason to withhold your data. We'll look in more detail at buying and selling online in Chapter 8.

You can also use technology to help protect you against spam. Most providers including AOL, Yahoo!, Google, Hotmail and BT.com offer a **spam** filter, which blocks emails that appear to be suspicious. The filter should prevent some emails from being delivered at all, while other suspect messages are automatically moved to a separate folder where you can delete them. These programmes are not foolproof, however, so you should always be cautious about opening emails from unfamiliar senders, and never click on an internet link within such an email or open an attachment sent with it. Watch closely for odd-looking addresses with strange spellings. **Phishing** emails often come from an address that is similar but not identical to a real company's name – even one extra character out of place should set alarm bells ringing. In any case, your own bank or insurance company will never send you an email asking you to disclose (or 'confirm') PINs, passwords or other personal information. Similarly, don't respond to unfamiliar emails that invite you to 'unsubscribe' from mailing lists. Doing so merely confirms that your email address is 'live' and therefore more valuable.

As a general rule, only give your email address to people or companies you trust. Do not publish your primary email address anywhere; clever programmes called 'spiders' comb the internet for email addresses that are then a prime target for spam. If you do need to publish an email address online, use a separate **webmail** account, which you can set up for free (with a provider such as Yahoo! or Hotmail) and keep your primary address for those you know.

One word of caution: spam filters can also catch legitimate email so you should check it regularly. Adding the email address of friends or colleagues to your address book means their messages should not be rejected.

If you use a wireless network to access your broadband connection, make sure you prevent others from also using it – or from hijacking your computer – if they are within geographical range. Unfortunately, the default encryption and access control settings on wireless network kits tend to be set to minimum to make them easier to set up. It is worth taking the time to reconfigure these and change any default passwords (which can be as obvious as 'password'). More on choosing 'strong' passwords later.

Make sure you regularly back up (save another copy of) your files. That way, if your computer is compromised, infected or stolen, you have not lost all the information (documents, photographs, music etc.) that was stored on it. You should not need to copy your operating system or software as you should have been supplied with original discs containing this information at the time of purchase.

Many anti-virus programmes contain a back-up facility, or you can buy separate software to manage the process. You can also copy files to a web-based back-up facility, or onto a portable hard drive that you simply plug into your computer. Make sure you store the backed-up material separately from your computer.

These techniques should help you protect your physical machine; now it is time to consider what else you can do to safeguard your personal data.

Your data: the threat to your privacy

The most valuable resource here is probably your common sense. That, coupled with a healthy dose of scepticism, will take you a long way.

Each time you set up an online account, you will have to provide various pieces of information that will be used to identify you when you log in. Normally there are several layers of security: a username or identification number (which may be generated automatically), plus a password or PIN, along with another memorable word or phrase (which you can normally choose yourself).

Think very carefully when setting these up. The goal is to choose something sufficiently memorable that you will not need to write it down anywhere, but which is not easy for anyone else to deduce.

It may sound too obvious to say it but never use 'password': you would be amazed at how many people do. You should also avoid using the names of your partner, children or pets as these are easily guessable. Ditto any of your dates of birth.

Many institutions suggest you might like to use your mother's maiden name. This is generally a bad idea since, depending on where and when you were born, this may be widely known or easily discoverable. You could adopt a completely different and unconnected name that you use only in these circumstances.

In any case, you should try to make all your passwords as 'strong' as possible. The best strategy is not to use a word at all, but a long string of characters (at least seven), which includes a combination of capital and lower case letters, numbers and symbols (such as ! ' £ $ @ etc.).

One trick is to think of a word that means something to you and then reverse it, replacing some of the letters with numbers and/or punctuation marks.

So Victoria might become A!rotc!V, Matthew Weh88aM, Shanghai $hangha1 and so on. Or you could insert a particular combination of three characters (i.e. &%*) at the beginning or end of the word – a simple but random strategy that is practically impossible to guess.

A word of caution – make sure you choose standard characters that will appear on any keyboard.

You should use different passwords for different accounts, otherwise a hacker who discovers one gains access to everything. It is also wise to change passwords and other memorable details regularly. At the very least, use separate passwords for financial sites, such as banks.

Never write any security information down. But if you must, be as cryptic as possible. So if your password is '$hangha1' because that's where you went on your honeymoon, don't write the name of the city but use 'honeymoon' or 'where we had noodles for the first time': something that will prompt you but not provide clues to anyone else.

Remember your bank can offer advice about staying safe online. It should never ask you to disclose your security information in an email or over the telephone. You may be asked to give one or two characters; never provide the full version. Beware of **phishing** emails.

Don't share your security information with friends or family either: disclosing details to a third party breaches the terms and conditions of most accounts, and you may find yourself unprotected if you were then to be a victim of fraud.

Some banks and building societies provide customers with extra security devices such as chip and PIN readers or code generators. Unfortunately, there is no common standard across these devices so, if you have online accounts with a number of different banks, you may have to use a number of these.

When logging into your accounts, make sure you type in the web address of your bank or other institution yourself. Never click on a link within an email or on another site unless you trust the source. When the login screen loads, look for **https** and the padlock in the address bar. If the site looks different, or the login procedure seems strange, check before proceeding. If in doubt, contact the company on an official customer services number to confirm whether anything has changed.

Check when the system says you last logged in: if this information is not accurate, someone else may have accessed your account in the meantime.

Never leave your computer unattended when you are logged into your account. Make sure you always log out on screen when you have finished; don't just close the window you are in because you may remain connected to the system.

Remember to take extra precautions when using public machines. These are detailed at the end of the previous chapter.

Read correspondence and statements from financial institutions carefully: report any suspicious transactions immediately. Make sure companies you deal with have your correct contact details. Don't ignore any unexpected post you receive – such as unsolicited credit cards – as they could be evidence of attempted or actual fraud.

Check your credit file with the UK's three credit reference agencies Equifax, Experian and Call Credit regularly – every 12 or 18 months or so. Each agency must provide a 'statutory' credit report for £2 although they will be delighted to charge you extra for a more detailed report. Beware – they sometimes also offer 'free' reports, which require you to sign up for a particular service that you then need to cancel to ensure you are not charged.

For more information, see: *www.equifax.co.uk, www.experian.co.uk* or *www.callcredit.co.uk/*.

Summary

It would be foolish to deny the risk we face when we connect to the internet or choose to manage our personal affairs online.

However, by following the steps outlined in this chapter – and using your common sense – you can protect both your computer and your personal information, leaving you to surf the web in safety and reap the rewards the internet can offer you.

Remember, if you have any questions or queries – or you suspect your security may have been compromised – contact your bank or other financial institution immediately. You will always be protected in the event of any fraud, as long as you can demonstrate you have not taken any risks with your data.

3
Banking

It is now possible to meet all of your banking needs via your computer. From current accounts to savings accounts to credit cards, ISAs and fixed rate bonds; all can be sourced, set up and managed online at any time of the day or night.

Internet banking allows you to view your balance, check statements, move money between accounts, pay your credit card and other bills, transfer payments to friends, manage direct debits and standing orders, and apply for other products. Many lenders will also let you view your mortgage account online.

Which bank?

All the major high street banks and a few building societies now offer internet access as standard. You may therefore be able simply to register for online access to your existing account(s), while still being able to use the branch network and telephone service. Some also offer internet-only accounts that you cannot operate in a branch.

In addition, there are a number of internet-only banks that do not have a branch network at all, although you may also be able to operate your account by phone or post.

The first step is to register; if you are opening a completely new account, you will need to provide proof of your identity and address. The bank may be able to verify your details electronically via the electoral roll or credit reference agencies, but you may be asked to send physical proof such as a recent utility bill or photocopy of your passport or driver's licence.

Existing customers should be able to request online access in the branch, over the telephone or via the website. You will then be allocated a username or customer number, and then asked to set up a number of further passwords or PINs to enable you to log in to your account.

See the previous chapter for advice about setting up 'strong' passwords, as well as lots of other tips about staying safe online.

Current accounts

As stated above, you could simply request online access to your present account. Alternatively, internet-only banks offering current accounts include Smile (part of the Co-operative), cahoot (part of Abbey), and First Direct (part of HSBC).

Internet current accounts offer the same functionality as their traditional counterparts: a cheque book, a debit/ATM card, the facility for direct debits and standing orders, and the ability to make electronic payments. Online customers have the added benefit of unfettered access to their account 24 hours a day, 7 days a week.

Despite the large number of current accounts available, very few customers tend to move. According to the Office of Fair Trading, which has been investigating the market, only 6% of customers it surveyed had switched accounts in the previous 12 months, one of the lowest rates in Europe.

The voluntary Banking Code, which governs the conduct of banks and building societies, sets out various minimum standards for switching: no charge, the old bank to give details of standing orders and direct debits etc. to the new bank within three working days, and the new bank to provide everything needed to use the account within ten working days of approving an application. Many banks have dedicated switching teams to manage the process for you.

The internet can be very useful to help you research current accounts if you are considering jumping ship. Financial comparison websites let you compare the level of interest paid on credit balances, the overdraft charges and fees, and other features such as free insurance or linked savings accounts.

Financial comparison websites are paid by banks or other institutions when people use their links to open accounts. Beware: some sites may not list all available accounts for their own commercial reasons, so it makes sense to use more than one. Well-known comparison services include: www.moneyfacts.co.uk, www.moneysupermarket.com and www.uswitch.com.

If you already have – or are considering opening – a so-called 'packaged' account, where in return for a monthly or annual fee you receive certain 'free' benefits such as travel insurance, car breakdown cover or credit card insurance, make sure the features are worth it. You might be better off opening a standard account and then shopping around to get competitive deals on the rest.

Faster payments

Online banking has been around for many years in the UK but, until recently, transfers initiated over the internet took the same frustrating three to four working days to arrive in a destination account as 'offline' transfers.

After many delays, a new 'Faster Payments' system finally began in May 2008, allowing customers to make payments of up to £10,000 via the internet (or over the phone) that arrive in the destination account within a maximum of two hours.

The new scheme was phased in gradually, but will eventually operate 24 hours a day, 7 days a week, between accounts belonging to its thirteen founding members. Standing orders between member banks can also be processed under the same-day framework on banking days.

The founder members are Abbey, Alliance and Leicester, Barclays, Citibank, Co-operative Bank, Clydesdale and Yorkshire Banks, HBOS, HSBC, Lloyds TSB, Nationwide Building Society, Northern Bank, Northern Rock and Royal Bank of

Scotland/NatWest. Other banks and building societies (including internet-only operations) are expected to join later.

For more information on Faster Payments, go to: www.apacs.org.uk/. You can check whether your present current account can receive Faster Payments at: www.apacs.org.uk/sortcodechecker.

Savings accounts

Internet-only banks have largely dominated the instant access savings market because their lower cost base has enabled them to offer competitive interest rates on a range of accounts, from instant access to cash ISAs to fixed rate bonds.

Many high street banks have launched their own online savings accounts in response. The highest paying National Savings and Investments Direct ISA is operated online and via the phone with no access via the Post Office.

Well-known internet-only banks include ICICI, and ING Direct. Such banks are regulated by the Financial Services Authority (FSA) in exactly the same way as traditional banks and building societies. For instance, when a number of Icelandic banks got into financial difficulties in 2008, the UK's regulatory procedures applied; albeit the government chose to offer greater protection to consumers than the letter of the law required. There's more on the safety of savings later in this chapter.

However, one important difference is that they are not 'clearing' banks, which means you need to set up a direct debit mandate through an existing current account to pay money into – and get money out of – such accounts. In practical terms this means there is a slight delay in accessing your money, although in time the new Faster Payments system may expand to include such banks.

Diabolical details

Whatever type of savings account you open (ISA, instant access, fixed rate), make sure you check the small print. As is so often the case with so many financial products, superficially attractive deals can have nasty surprises lurking in the small print.

Beware the introductory bonus: Interest rates on new accounts are often boosted for 6 or 12 months, propelling them to the top of the rate tables. But once the bonus is removed, the account can plummet like a lead balloon. Bonuses aren't bad: you just need to be clear about when they end – at which point you may wish to find a better paying account. Why not put a reminder in your calendar when you open the account?

Guaranteed? Some accounts link the level of interest rate paid to the Bank of England's base rate. The promise may be to exceed, match or remain a fixed amount beneath it, usually for a set period. Such certainty can be very attractive.

Am I eligible? Many accounts require you to deposit a certain amount, either to open the account at all, or to qualify for higher interest rates. Others require a minimum balance. Some have age criteria – over 50s accounts have become very popular.

Do I need to have another account? Some high paying online accounts are restricted to existing holders of other accounts, such as a particular current account. Several attractive cash ISAs require people to open more complicated (and potentially riskier) investment products at the same time. In such a situation, make sure all components of a product are suitable for you.

How can I get my money? Some accounts will only pay a certain rate if you stick to a limited number of withdrawals per year: exceed the quota and the rate can fall sharply. Other accounts don't pay any interest for the month in which you make a withdrawal. You can sometimes get a higher rate if you open a 'notice' account, where you receive your money 30, 60 or 90 days after requesting it.

Is my money locked away for a set period? Similarly, you can often get an even better interest rate if you are prepared to make a commitment for one, two or three years. But in many cases, your cash really is unavailable before the end of the term without significant penalties, which can wipe out most – or even all – of the interest you expected to earn. If you might need access to your money, don't sign it away.

Regular habits: Many banks offer so-called 'regular saver' accounts with more favourable rates if you save money every month. However, you are usually limited to one deposit per month, typically capped at around £250. So although your balance does attract a high interest rate, it only ever applies to a relatively small balance. These accounts usually last for one or two years, after which your money tends to be transferred into another account paying significantly less. The interest rate can also drop sharply if you miss a monthly payment; and access before the end of the term is normally restricted. Such accounts can work well if you want to save less than the maximum and can make a commitment to pay every month – but if you have a lump sum, you would actually earn more interest if you put the whole amount in a lower-paying account at the outset.

Do I need to pay tax? Since April 2008 it has been possible to save up to £3,600 – or half the total annual ISA allowance – in a cash ISA. But non-taxpayers can register to receive the interest on *any* savings account 'gross' – i.e. without tax deducted. You need to fill out HM Revenue & Customs (HMRC) form R85 for each bank or building society where you have accounts. For more information, phone 0845 980 0645 or go to: *www.hmrc.gov.uk/taxback*.

As with current accounts, financial comparison websites will let you evaluate different products to help identify the one that's right for you. Well-known commercial comparison sites listing savings accounts include: *www.moneyfacts.co.uk, www.moneyexpert.com, www.moneyextra.com* and *www.moneysupermarket.com.* Again, it's always worth using more than one. To help you choose a product that has remained consistently competitive, Moneyfacts will also let you compare the best performing savings accounts over the previous 18 or 36 months.

In addition, the Financial Services Authority produces comparison tables for a number of products including savings accounts on its website at: *www.fsa.gov.uk/tables*. The FSA's tables are completely objective.

Savings protection

The recent financial turmoil has brought sharply into focus the limitations of the protection for cash deposits. The Financial Services Compensation Scheme (FSCS) had been in operation for several years but was poorly understood until the collapse of Northern Rock in September 2007.

In the immediate aftermath, the government increased the amount of compensation available to 100% of the first £35,000 of total deposits held by an individual per institution and subsequently increased the limit to *£50,000 per individual per institution*. The FSCS makes no distinction between high street and internet-only banks.

However, stung into action by footage of thousands of anxious Northern Rock customers queuing outside branches in an attempt to withdraw their savings, the government put in place a separate total guarantee for all funds held on deposit with the bank.

Similarly, when the internet bank Icesave – the UK branch of the Icelandic bank Landsbanki – was declared in default in October 2008, the Chancellor announced that no retail customers would lose any money as a result of its collapse.

At the same time, the government also arranged to transfer all the retail customers of other failed Icelandic banks to the Dutch online bank ING Direct.

For its part, the Irish government unilaterally announced that it would fully safeguard all deposits, bonds and debts in six banks and building societies for two years until September 2010.

It therefore seems highly unlikely that – during the present financial crisis at least – the UK government would be prepared to allow any retail bank to collapse and leave customers out of pocket beyond the limits of the statutory protection.

However, such a situation will not continue indefinitely and therefore it is important that you understand what the position would be should you ever have to make a claim under the FSCS's normal rules.

The £50,000 limit applies to capital and interest; so if you deposit £50,000 none of the interest would be protected because it would be above the limit. You can get round this by withdrawing the interest or arranging for it to be paid directly into a separate account with a different bank.

Joint account holders are assumed to hold an equal share of deposited funds, meaning the first £100,000 in a joint account would be protected.

Kate *and* **Jonathan** *had £120,000 in a joint savings account. If their bank collapsed, they would each be entitled to £50,000 compensation, but the remaining £20,000 would not be protected.*

If a customer also has a loan or mortgage with the same bank or building society, this would be deducted from the savings total before any compensation would be paid.

Conrad *has £50,000 in savings and a loan of £15,000 with the same bank. If it were to collapse, he would be entitled to compensation of £50,000 – £15,000 = £35,000. If Diggory had £100,000 in savings and a mortgage of £70,000, again with the same bank, he would be entitled to £100,000 – £70,000 = £30,000.*

The £50,000 limit applies per 'authorised institution', but what constitutes an authorised institution is not straightforward.

Some banks are authorised with the Financial Services Authority at a group level, meaning that the £50,000 limit would apply across all the different banks in that group. Therefore, if that group failed, the maximum amount a customer could claim would be £50,000, even if he or she had less than the limit in separate accounts with three different providers belonging to the parent company.

In contrast, some other banking groups authorise

each individual bank as separate entities, in which case the £50,000 limit would apply to each one.

For clarification, contact your provider or check the authorisation position with the Financial Services Authority Consumer Helpline on 0845 606 1234 or at: www.fsa.gov.uk.

An institution's corporate structure is also relevant to the protection given to money saved with non-UK banks. Banks from outside the European Economic Area (EEA), which operate in the UK, are authorised here in the same way as their UK counterparts and offer their savers identical protection.

However, some European banks operate in the UK under something called the 'passport scheme'. This means that, in the event of a collapse, the bank's home country's compensation scheme would be initially responsible for paying compensation according to its own limits. The FSCS would then top up compensation to the UK level of £50,000. Effectively, you should have the same level of protection but it could be more complicated to have to claim twice.

In reality, though, such distinctions may prove irrelevant. Icesave's parent company Landsbanki was a member of the passport scheme but, in the event of its collapse, there was not enough money in the Icelandic protection scheme to meet its obligations to its UK customers, so the UK government simply bypassed the system altogether.

It is not clear how long the government will be willing (or able) to stand behind 100% of customer deposits with institutions that run into difficulty but it would certainly be foolish to assume such extraordinary guarantees will remain in place indefinitely. It is, therefore, wise to ensure you understand the limits of the rules as they were intended to – and may yet – be applied.

For further information, you may find the following links useful:

- HM Treasury: *www.hm-treasury.gov.uk*
- Financial Services Authority: *www.fsa.gov.uk*
- Financial Services Compensation Scheme: *www.fscs.org.uk*
- FSCS list of firms which have topped up their protection: *www.fscs.org.uk/consumer/ how_to_claim/deposits/eea_firms_that_have_ topped_up/*
- Irish government's Deposit Guarantee Scheme: *www.finance.gov.ie/.*

Summary

Technology means it is now possible to do all your banking via your computer. Whether you arrange internet access to your present 'bricks and mortar' bank or place your money with an internet-only institution, your current and savings accounts, ISAs and credit cards can all be sourced, set up and managed online at your convenience.

The web can also be extremely useful in letting you compare the hundreds (sometimes thousands) of products on the market. Banking online may save you money; but, as with any account, you should check the small print to make sure you have the correct product for your circumstances. Just like their branch-based cousins, internet accounts can be uncompetitive and misleading.

So far the government has intervened to protect consumer deposits when banks have failed, but, in theory, only the first £50,000 is guaranteed, so make sure you understand exactly what protection the Financial Services Compensation Scheme would offer you and consider spreading your money between a number of differently authorised institutions.

---------------- 4 ----------------

Investing

Just as the internot can be an extremely useful tool to help you manage your savings, it can also help you organise your investments, from individual company shares and ISAs to investment funds and unit trusts. Depending on how your pension is structured, you may also be able to manage its underlying investments online as well.

In addition, you will find a multitude of websites offering information and interactive analytical tools to help you decide how and where to invest.

However, by its very nature, investment is risky, and it is not suitable for everyone. Nor are all investment products right for every investor. Furthermore, all investments should be considered as long-term projects, i.e. at least five to ten years.

The internet allows you to buy and sell investments directly without financial advice. But this is not for the faint-hearted or inexperienced. Going it alone means you have little or no comeback if your investments perform poorly, so you should be very cautious about going down this route.

 PLEASE NOTE, this chapter will only offer a very basic introduction to some of the options for investing online: you should

consider taking detailed individual financial advice before making any decisions.

First things first

When you invest, you are taking a calculated risk that you will get more money back than you put in. But, in most cases, returns are not guaranteed and you may not get back all or any of the money you invest.

Different investment products contain different levels of risk, which is why it is important to diversify, to spread your money across a range of investments and assets such as shares, bonds, cash and property. Diversification – also known as asset allocation – can help you reduce the level of risk you are taking but cannot remove it altogether.

You should not, therefore, invest money that you could not afford to lose, or at the least leave tied up for a reasonable period. It is also a good idea to consider your finances in the round before making any investment decisions.

It would not normally make sense to start investing if you are paying off short-term debts such as credit cards or personal loans. Deal with these first. Similarly, you should ensure you have some easily accessible 'emergency' cash savings before you begin putting money away for the longer term.

Many experts suggest you should have sufficient cash savings to cover at least three months' essential outgoings. The

*Financial Services Authority's consumer
website Money Made Clear has a budget
calculator to help you work out how
much you might need:
www.moneymadeclear.fsa.gov.uk/tools/
budget_calculator.*

Even if you feel confident about making
investment decisions on your own, it is a good
idea to pay for a session with a financial adviser to
help clarify your strategy before you begin. There
will be more on financial advice below.

How to invest

Once you have decided you want to invest, there
are a number of routes open to you. You can buy
investments directly from an investment company,
a life insurance company, a bank or building
society, a friendly society or via a stockbroker or
financial adviser.

The Financial Services Authority (FSA) regulates
companies that sell or advise on investments,
which means they and their advisers are supposed
to meet certain standards. Dealing with a
regulated firm also gives you access to a formal
complaints procedure and a compensation system
should the investment company itself fail.

*You can check a firm's regulatory status
on the FSA's register at:
www.fsa.gov.uk/register.*

Shares

When you buy an individual company's shares, you are buying an actual part of that firm. If the business does well, the value of the shares will rise, giving you the option to sell them for more than you paid, thereby making a profit. In addition, some companies make regular payments, called dividends, to their shareholders. Of course, there is no guarantee that a company will succeed and you may find the value of your shares falls well below what you paid for them.

Find out more about shares from the London Stock Exchange's Investor Centre at: www.londonstockexchange.com.

Shares are usually bought and sold via a stockbroker – even financial advisers and investment managers deal through a stockbroker. There are three main types of service on offer with varying costs:

Advisory: The stockbroker assesses your individual circumstances, comes up with an investment strategy for you and makes suggestions about buying and selling specific shares.

COST: Under this model you will either be charged a fee or commission for the provision of the advice. If you ask the adviser to arrange the purchase or sale of shares, you will be charged separately, usually a fixed percentage of the size of the transaction (commission), plus associated dealing costs.

Discretionary: The stockbroker assesses your individual circumstances and devises a strategy, but buys and sells shares in your portfolio without consulting you first.

COST: This is the most expensive service as you are paying for advice, active management of your portfolio plus the actual costs of dealing (commission and other associated fees).

Execution-only: The stockbroker simply buys or sells shares at your request, offering no advice about the wisdom or otherwise of your decision. The internet has played a crucial role in the development of this model. There are dozens of online execution-only brokers that allow you to buy and sell shares on the web at a fraction of the cost of traditional stockbrokers, making it economically viable to buy and sell on a much smaller scale than in the past. In fact, many leading stockbrokers now also have execution-only arms which operate alongside (but entirely separately from) their main business.

COST: The cheapest service. You simply pay the actual costs of dealing, which are much lower than the fees or commission payable for the Advisory or Discretionary services. Some companies also levy an additional administration fee (usually small).

One way to learn about investing directly in shares is to join forces with friends or relatives and set up a share club. Find out more from Proshare at: www.proshareclubs.co.uk.

Pooled or collective investments

These involve lots of people putting different amounts of money into a pooled fund, which is then invested in a number of shares and other assets by a fund manager. You own a portion of this fund according to how much you have invested. There are various potential advantages to investing this way compared to buying individual shares. You hope to benefit from the fund manager's professional expertise, you spread your risk by putting your money into a range of different companies and assets, you take advantage of cheaper dealing costs when buying and selling, and the fund manager handles the administration of looking after your investments in return for an annual management fee (and sometimes also an initial fee levied when you first put money in).

There is an enormous range of pooled investments available, including unit trusts, investment trusts, life assurance policies and open-ended investment companies (OEICs). Most investments are structured around a particular theme, which could be geographical (e.g. European, Far East), sector specific (e.g. defence, banking, utility firms) or size-related (e.g. large/mid/small cap, short for 'capitalised value').

Others simply follow – or 'track' – particular stock market indexes, such as the FTSE 100, FTSE All-Share or the NASDAQ.

Fees vary between different types of collective investments as well as between different providers. The way you choose to buy your investment can also have a bearing on what it costs you.

Find out more about pooled investments from the FSA's Money Made Clear website at: www.moneymadeclear.fsa.gov.uk/ products/investments/types/ pooled_investments.html.

As with shares, there are a number of ways to buy collective investments.

Financial adviser: The adviser assesses your individual circumstances, comes up with an investment strategy for you and recommends specific collective investments to you. You should be given written 'Key Features' information about the investment products the adviser recommends, explaining why he or she believes they are suitable for you. Not all advisers offer products from the whole of the market; make sure you understand the context in which your adviser operates.

COST: Some advisers will charge a fee for this advice, some will take commission from the company that operates the investment, while others will use a combination of the two. The cost of the

advice must be disclosed to you, along
with any initial and ongoing charges levied
by the investment provider.

*Find out more about financial advice in
general from the FSA's Money Made
Clear website at:
www.moneymadeclear.fsa.gov.uk/guides/
advice/getting_financial_advice.html.*

Direct: You identify a particular investment and
buy it directly from the insurance company or
investment fund group. They must provide clear
information about the product's Key Features and
details about charges, but do not have to check
whether a particular investment is right for you. If
you buy a product this way and it turns out to be
unsuitable, as long as the information you were
given was accurate, you have no comeback.

*COST: In most cases you will be charged
an upfront fee and an annual fee thereafter.
These vary but are typically around 3–5%
for upfront charges and 1–1.5% for annual
management charges. Because these fees
are fixed, buying directly is ironically often
the most expensive way to buy investment
products.*

*Find out more from the Investment
Management Association at:
www.investmentuk.org; The Association
of Investment Companies:
www.theaic.co.uk; and the Association of
British Insurers: www.abi.org.uk.*

Fund supermarkets: These are internet-only operations which offer investors a 'one-stop shop' to buy products from a wide range of different fund managers and investment companies. You can then manage your portfolio of different investments online in one place, tracking performance history etc. As with the execution-only stockbrokers already discussed (several firms offer both services), you will not receive any advice about your investment decisions, although many fund supermarkets do offer detailed research and highly sophisticated analytical tools.

COST: The real beauty of fund supermarkets is the price. Under this model, fund supermarkets discount most or all of the upfront and annual management fees that you pay if you buy via an adviser or direct from the company itself. Hence fund supermarkets are also known as 'discount brokers'. Some specialist discount brokers will even rebate future commission if you transfer existing investments to them.

Fund supermarkets are particularly useful if you want to buy investments within a tax-free stocks and shares ISA 'wrapper'. You can easily switch your ISA money between different qualifying investments and/or providers without losing your tax-free status. You also benefit from the lower charges offered by fund supermarkets. Since April 2008 you have been able to invest up to £7,200 in a stocks and shares ISA per year. You can also transfer money held in cash ISAs taken out in previous tax years into stocks and shares ISAs without using up any of the current year's allowance.

Find out more about ISAs at: www.hmrc.gov.uk/leaflets/isa.htm or by phoning HMRC's ISA helpline on 0845 604 1701.

A number of fund supermarkets also offer *self-invested personal pensions* (or SIPPs). A SIPP is a pension 'wrapper' designed to hold the money invested for your retirement, which lets you move it between different assets and providers as you wish. As before, the fund supermarket lets you manage your investment online. SIPP charges can be higher than more traditional pensions but, as with non-pension investments, some fund supermarkets offer extremely competitive deals on charges. **Beware: SIPPs are only suitable for highly experienced investors**.

Find out more about SIPPs from the FSA's Money Made Clear website at: www.moneymadeclear.fsa.gov.uk/ products/pensions/types/ self-invested_personal_pensions.htm and the Pensions Advisory Service website at www.pensionsadvisoryservice.org.uk/ specialist_pension_arrangements/sipp.

Bonds

With a bond you lend money to a company, local authority or the government (in which case the bond is known as a gilt) in return for an IOU. Unlike most investments, bonds are not designed to achieve capital growth but instead offer a fixed rate of interest each year plus the return of the capital at the end of a specified period – i.e. a '7% Treasury 2021' is a gilt issued by the Treasury, which pays 7% interest per year and is repayable in 2021

However, you don't need to hold a bond or gilt until its redemption date as they can be traded just like shares. That means their value can rise and fall in line with supply and demand.

Gilt prices tend to rise when interest rates fall and inflation is low, since a guarantee of 7% interest during those circumstances is more valuable than if interest rates are at a similar level.

Investing in bonds is generally considered to be lower risk than investing directly in shares. Gilts, in particular, are deemed very low risk since the UK government has never failed to repay its investors. With corporate bonds there is a greater risk that the company may default on its interest payments or fail to return the capital and, therefore, the interest rate on these bonds tends to be higher than that on gilts.

You can buy corporate bonds via a stockbroker. If you don't want to buy bonds directly, you can still put money into collective investments, which invest in a range of corporate and government bonds, again via stockbrokers, financial advisers or fund supermarkets. Charges will vary according to your route.

You can buy gilts through stockbrokers and some high street banks, all of whom will charge commission on the purchase. Alternatively, you can buy them directly from the government's Debt Management Office (DMO) through a gilt auction, subject to minimum purchase rules. In order to access this option you need to become a member of the DMO's 'Approved Group of Investors'. There is no commission charged on gilts bought at auction.

Approved investors can also use the DMO's Retail Gift Purchase and Sale service to buy and sell gilts via its agent Computershare Investor Services. Computershare's charges may be lower than a stockbroker's.

 Find out more at: www.dmo.gov.uk or: www-uk.computershare.com/Investor/ Gilts.

Some useful contacts
Financial advisers/stockbrokers
- IFA Promotion: *www.unbiased.co.uk*
- My Local Adviser: *www.mylocaladviser.co.uk*
- Find an Adviser: *www.findanadviser.org*
- Institute of Financial Planning: *www.financialplanning.org.uk*
- Association of Private Client Investment Managers and Stockbrokers: *www.apcims.co.uk*
- London Stock Exchange: Locate a Broker: *www.londonstockexchange.com.*

Companies offering online share dealing
- Self Trade: *www.selftrade.co.uk*

- E*trade: *www.etrade.co.uk*
- TD Waterhouse: *www.tdwaterhouse.co.uk*
- Barclays Stockbrokers:
  www.barclays-stockbrokers.co.uk
- The Share Centre: *www.share.co.uk*
- Halifax Share Dealing:
  www.halifax.co.uk/sharedealing
- Redmayne Bentley: *www.redmayne.co.uk.*

Fund supermarkets/discount brokers

- Fidelity Funds Network: *www.fidelity.co.uk*
- Funds Direct: *www.fundsdirect.co.uk*
- Cofunds: *www.cofunds.co.uk*
- Cavendish Online: *www.cavendishonline.co.uk*
- Hargreaves Lansdown: *www.h-l.co.uk*
- Chartwell: *investorcentre.chartwell.co.uk.*

Gilts

- Debt Management Office: *www.dmo.gov.uk*
- Computer Share: *www-uk.computershare.com/
  Investor/Gilts.*

What protection do investments have?

Investing money is risky: in almost every case, neither the return nor the initial capital is guaranteed. If you invest £20,000 in the stock market but find that it is only worth £10,000 at the point you need to sell, you would not automatically be entitled to any compensation. To that end, then, money that you invest is not protected at all.

Similarly, if you bought an investment product without financial advice – i.e. from an execution-only broker – and it turned out to be unsuitable, you would not qualify for any redress.

However, if you bought the product *after* taking financial advice from a regulated adviser, and it was not appropriate for you – perhaps because it was riskier than you were told or a crucial condition was not disclosed – then you *may* be entitled to compensation.

In the first instance, you should complain to the firm that sold you the product, which should investigate and respond within eight weeks. If you were still not happy, you could take your complaint to the Financial Ombudsman, a free and impartial complaints resolution service.

Generally the Ombudsman tries to put customers back in the position they would be in if whatever went wrong had not gone wrong. This *might* include ordering a firm to pay you compensation. The Ombudsman's findings are binding on the firm in question although you can choose to take your case to court if you disagree.

If you cannot contact the firm in question because it is no longer trading, you might be able to get help from the Financial Services Compensation Scheme (FSCS). However, the FSCS can only pay compensation in very clearly defined circumstances and up to a specified limit – £48,000 per person for an investment claim (100% of the first £30,000 and 90% of the next £20,000).

Find out more about complaining about a firm at:
www.moneymadeclear.fsa.gov.uk/guides/complaints/making_a_complaint.html.

There is more about the Financial Ombudsman Service at: www.financial-ombudsman.org.uk.

Read more about compensation from the Financial Services Compensation Scheme at: www.fscs.org.uk.

Find out more

As well as allowing you to buy and sell certain products online, the internet is a tremendous source of useful information about all aspects of investment. It is – of course – also a source of much that is unreliable and untrustworthy, so always attempt to verify information before you act on it.

You may find the following websites of interest:

Official

- Financial Services Authority Money Made Clear: Investment: www.moneymadeclear.fsa.gov.uk/products/investments/investments.html
- London Stock Exchange: www.londonstockexchange.com.

Professional organisations

- Investment Management Association: *www.investmentuk.org*
- Association of Investment Companies: *www.theaic.co.uk*

- Association of Private Client Investment Managers and Stockbrokers: *www.apcims.co.uk*
- Association of British Insurers: *www.abi.org.uk*
- Proshare: *www.proshareclubs.co.uk.*

Information

- FTSE: *www.ftse.com*
- Financial Times: *www.ft.com*
- Bloomberg: *www.bloomberg.com*
- Citywire: *www.citywire.co.uk*
- Trust Net: *www.trustnet.com*
- Morning Star: *www.morningstar.co.uk*
- The Motley Fool: *www.fool.co.uk*
- Ethical Investment Research Service: *www.eiris.org.*

Summary

As in so many aspects of finance, the internet is a powerful tool that has revolutionised the investment world. The innovative execution-only brokers and fund supermarkets discussed in this chapter simply would not – could not – exist without the web.

In the same way that these companies have challenged the traditional stockbroking business model, the numerous websites offering financial data and analysis have helped democratise investment by making publicly and freely available that which was previously jealously guarded.

But as we said at the beginning of this chapter, investing money carries risk and should not be done lightly or thought of as a short-term venture. Similarly, not every share tip posted on a financial website should be believed or relied upon.

Technology will let you go far alone but only experience can tell you whether you are skilled enough to take advantage of this brave new investment world.

5

Insurance

The insurance market has also been revolutionised by the web. Many companies offer special discounts to online customers. As with banking, there are some firms that only operate on the internet. And an increasing number of incredibly sophisticated sites let you search the market and compare thousands of different insurance policies in minutes.

However you buy your insurance – directly from a particular company, by going to a broker or independent financial adviser (IFA), or via a price comparison site – the internet can play a key role in helping to identify the most suitable policy for your needs, as well as offering a wealth of information about what is available.

Generally firms that sell insurance and those that underwrite the insured risk are regulated by the Financial Services Authority (FSA) or are themselves agents of a regulated company. That means they must meet certain standards and consumers can call on statutory complaints and compensation procedures. It is therefore crucial to ensure any company you deal with over the internet is actually regulated by the UK authorities.

 You can check a firm's regulatory status on the FSA's register at: www.fsa.gov.uk/register/

There is one notable exception: extended warranties (such as for electrical appliances) sold alongside goods are not covered by the FSA's regime.

Before we look at the different ways you can buy insurance, it seems sensible to run through some general points, which could help you reduce your premiums.

Top tips

1. If you can, pay your premium in one lump sum; many insurers charge you interest for the privilege of paying monthly. Also, consider agreeing to a larger 'excess' in the event of a claim.

2. Remember, your buildings insurance only needs to cover the cost of rebuilding your property and not the value of the land itself. There is a useful calculator to help you work out the level of cover you need at: *www.bcis.co.uk/RebuildingCosts.*

3. Avoid mortgage deals that compel you to take the lender's own buildings insurance because premiums may rise substantially in subsequent years, leaving you trapped. You can often make additional savings by buying a combined buildings and contents policy, but check that the details of each part meet your needs.

4. Many insurers offer a standard level of contents cover. To clarify how much you actually need, compile a list of everything you own (including gifts) with the approximate

date and value and calculate the total. If your reckoning is substantially below the limit you are being offered, try to negotiate for less cover and a cheaper premium.

5. Boost your security: fit a burglar alarm, add window locks, upgrade your door locks, put in security lighting, join your local neighbourhood watch scheme, install and regularly test smoke alarms, insulate pipes and tanks.

6. Consider choosing indemnity insurance for your contents cover. This replaces goods with those of the same age. This is much cheaper than a 'new for old' policy, which will pay for a brand new substitute, but make sure you understand what you would get in the event of a claim.

7. While additional named drivers normally increase the cost, younger drivers can sometimes save by adding an older and more experienced driver to their policy. Younger men can lower their premium by including a female partner.

8. UK residents aged 16 plus who possess a European Health Insurance Card (EHIC) are entitled to free or reduced cost state-provided healthcare when on holiday within the European Economic Area (the EU countries plus Iceland, Liechtenstein and Norway) and Switzerland. Find out more at: *www.ehic.org.*

9. If you do not have any dependents, such as partner, spouse or children, you may not need life insurance.

10. Be very cautious before taking out protection policies such as critical illness cover, payment protection insurance (PPI) – also sometimes known as 'accident, sickness and unemployment' or ASU – mortgage payment protection insurance (MPPI) and income protection – also called permanent health insurance (PHI). These polices can be useful. However, they are complex and have a vast number of exclusions and restrictions. You can find out lots more about this kind of insurance on the FSA's consumer website at: *www.moneymadeclear.fsa.gov.uk/pdfs/ insurance.pdf* and compare different PPI or MPPI providers at: *www.fsa.gov.uk/tables.*

And finally, don't just automatically renew your policy with the same insurer every year. Put a date in your calendar six weeks before your policy expires and spend some time shopping around. At the very least, ask your provider if it is prepared to match the quotes you find elsewhere.

You can find lots more useful general information about insurance at: Directgov: *www.direct.gov.uk/ en/MoneyTaxAndBenefits/ManagingMoney/ Insurance* and the Association of British Insurers: *www.abi.org.uk/.*

To be advised or not to be advised

If you are buying or renewing your home or car insurance, you may be happy to go straight to one of the large insurers or another institution like your bank or even your supermarket. Many offer enticing discounts to new or existing online customers.

All firms that sell insurance directly to consumers without offering any advice still have to follow the FSA's rules. But remember, in most cases, such companies only sell their own insurance policies; their staff are salespeople and not advisers, and they are not able to offer you any independent advice.

That matters because, if you buy an insurance product without taking advice, you are responsible for deciding whether it is appropriate for your circumstances. If it turns out to be unsuitable, you may have fewer grounds for complaint against the firm than if you had used a broker or financial adviser.

Given the complexity of life and protection insurance policies, it is wise to seek specialist independent financial advice before deciding whether and which to buy.

Find out more about financial advice in general from the Financial Services Authority: *www.moneymadeclear.fsa.gov.uk/ guides/advice/getting_financial_advice.html*.

How to find a broker

Most brokers tend to see clients face to face or talk to them over the telephone, but the internet can prove invaluable in helping you to find an adviser and guiding you about what you should expect from them.

The following websites will put you in touch with a local broker or financial adviser:

- British Insurance Brokers' Association (BIBA): *www.biba.org.uk*
- Institute of Insurance Brokers: *www.iib-uk.com*
- IFA Promotion: *www.unbiased.co.uk*
- My Local Adviser: *www.mylocaladviser.co.uk*
- Find an Adviser: *www.findanadviser.org*
- Institute of Financial Planning: *www.financialplanning.org.uk.*

 You can specify the level of expertise you wish your broker or adviser to have. If you want a life insurance specialist, ask for one.

Under the FSA's rules, brokers and advisers who make recommendations based on their assessment of your personal circumstances must only recommend products that are suitable for you. It is therefore imperative that you answer any questions fully and accurately. Failure to do so may invalidate future claims, and prevent you from complaining if you are subsequently sold an inappropriate policy.

In return, advisers have to provide you with certain statutory information. You should be given two standard 'Keyfacts' documents. The first should confirm that the firm is authorised by the FSA to sell insurance, whether it offers advice or information, how it charges for its services and whether it offers products from the entire market or from a limited range of providers.

If you are being sold so-called general insurance (i.e. a non-investment product), you should also be given an additional document summarising the policy's main features and costs, including any significant limits or restrictions. For investment insurance products, this should be a more detailed publication including an illustration of how the policy might perform in the future.

It may be tempting merely to glance through this paperwork but it is crucial that you read it carefully. Failure to check could mean you end up buying an inappropriate policy, which does not offer the protection you think you have paid for.

You can change your mind and get your money back within a certain period (usually 14 or 30 days) after arranging any insurance contract.

Comparison websites

Comparison sites are like highly sophisticated search engines that let you compare hundreds – sometimes thousands – of different policies. The idea is that you set up an online account with a comparison site, giving it your personal details and the relevant information necessary to generate a quote from an insurance company.

The website submits that information to lots of different providers simultaneously, and then presents you with a list of quotations for you to consider and compare. They are normally ranked by price but you can sort by other criteria that are important to you.

You can then simply click on the policy you want, or change some or all of the details submitted – e.g.

increase a voluntary excess or change the type of car – and request new quotations. The comparison site saves your personal details and the quotations that have been generated, allowing you to retrieve the information later by logging in again.

These sites can be an incredibly useful tool but it's important to be clear about the service they provide. Comparison websites do not offer advice; they merely supply information to consumers and, although the quotations that they generate may be ranked according to price, this does not constitute a recommendation. The responsibility for wading through the small print to ensure that the policy is suitable belongs solely to you.

If you decide to buy a policy, your contract is with the insurer, not the third party in the middle and, if that policy turns out to be unsuitable, as long as the information provided to you was accurate, you are likely to have little or no comeback against the website.

Not all insurance companies deal with comparison websites; no comparison site deals with all insurers, so make sure you understand the range of providers whose products you are being offered. Some price comparison sites accept payments to place certain products higher in the results table – if you are in any doubt, ask the comparison site to clarify its policy.

Consumer bodies have expressed concern that some comparison websites are not clear enough about the level of excess that applies to the policies they list. Sites have also come under fire for not spelling out the assumptions they make about customers' circumstances. Using some assumptions can speed up the process of obtaining quotations, but if these do not accurately represent your situation, you may end up with the wrong product. So if in doubt, check. Answer every question you are posed as fully as possible.

Once you have received a list of quotations, don't just be led by price. Some companies have been accused of reducing the level of cover they offer in order to appear cheaper in the table of quotations. Choosing the cheapest policy without checking the detail of what's included could mean you are not as comprehensively covered as you think – or even leave you without any cover at all.

There are many insurance comparison sites, but here are the most popular:

- Money Supermarket: *www.moneysupermarket.com*
- Go Compare: *www.gocompare.com*
- Confused.com: *www.confused.com*
- Tesco Compare: *www.tescocompare.com*
- Compare the Market: *www.comparethemarket.com*
- uSwitch: *www.uswitch.com*.

As no site covers the whole market, it is a good idea to enter your details into a number of sites so you can compare the different quotations.

Summary

Whether you buy your insurance directly from a particular company, by going to a broker or independent financial adviser (IFA), or via a price comparison site, the internet can help you find the most suitable policy for your needs, as well as offering a great deal of useful information about what's available. At the very least it can help you collect some quotes, which you can challenge your present insurer to match.

But remember, the web cannot do all the work for you. Don't rely solely on any one comparison site, and make sure you understand exactly what is – and is not – covered under any policy. Buying direct may save you money but it also means you bear all the responsibility if the policy you buy turns out to be wrong for your situation, which is something you may not discover until the moment when your claim is rejected.

6

Utility bills

The internet can also help you get a better deal on your utility bills. Some energy providers offer exclusive online tariffs, and – as with insurance – sophisticated comparison websites can help you to weigh up the merits and prices of different offers and then to switch suppliers.

In addition, there is a lot of advice on the web about how to reduce your bills through, for instance, energy- and water-saving measures. You can also find information to help you compare and switch telephone, mobile and broadband providers.

Energy

Since the energy market was opened up to competition in 1999, around half of all customers have switched their supplier, typically saving about £100 a year. However, the biggest savings tend to be made on the first switch; you can continue to move to new providers as you wish but the financial benefit is likely to reduce.

You can find lots of general information about switching energy companies at: *www.ofgem.gov.uk/ Consumers.*

You can approach a new supplier directly but the majority of people who have switched have done so via energy comparison websites.

Customers provide their postcode, current supplier and tariff, information about their usage and payment method (i.e. direct debit, quarterly bills etc.). The sites then rank the various energy deals available by price. Whether the deal you select is an 'online' tariff or not, you can apply for it via the switching website itself.

The new supplier then manages the process, confirming the switch date directly to you. Customers should take a meter reading at that point to enable them to settle the final bill with their old provider, cancelling any direct debits or standing orders if necessary.

Any energy customers who are not in debt to their supplier can switch to a new provider, although not all comparison sites allow prepayment meter customers to switch online.

The consumer watchdog energywatch launched a voluntary code of practice for price comparison sites in 2002. A revised 'Confidence Code' was launched in October 2008 by energywatch's successor, Consumer Focus. Go to: *www.consumerfocus.org.uk.*

The following price comparison sites are accredited under the code and display the Consumer Focus logo:

- Switch with Which?: *www.switchwithwhich.com*
- Unravelit: *www.unravelit.com*
- Home Advisory Service: *www.homeadvisoryservice.co.uk*
- Simply Switch: www.simplyswitch.com

- Confused.com: www.confused.com
- uSwitch: www.uswitch.com
- The Energy Shop: www.theenergyshop.com
- UK Power: www.ukpower.co.uk
- Energy Helpline: www.energyhelpline.com
- Save On Your Bills: www.saveonyourbills.co.uk
- Energylinx: www.energylinx.co.uk.

Remember, not all the sites offer deals from every provider, so you may wish to run your details through more than one.

Cut your bill

As well as switching supplier, there are many other ways to save money.

1. Pay by direct debit.
2. Opt for a combined 'dual fuel' deal where you take electricity and gas from the same supplier.
3. Install cavity wall insulation, loft insulation, double glazing, lag your hot water tank and pipes and/or invest in a new boiler. Draught-proof your windows and doors. Fit thermostatic valves to your radiators to allow you to control the heat of individual rooms. Turn down the thermostat by one degree.
4. Use energy efficient light bulbs. Switch televisions or DVD players off instead of leaving them on 'standby'. Use the lowest temperature programmes in your washing machine and dishwasher that you can. Defrost your freezer regularly to ensure it runs efficiently.
5. Ensure any new household appliances are marked 'Energy Saving Recommended' or

have a European energy label rating of A or higher.

Find lots more useful advice at: *www.energysavingtrust.org.uk* or phone 0800 512 012 and *www.direct.gov.uk/actonco2.*

More help

There are a number of grants and offers available towards the installation costs of many of the energy efficiency measures listed above. There are three main sources of help: government, local authorities and the energy industry itself. Find out more at: *www.energysavingtrust.org.uk/gid.*

Government

While those on benefits – such as disability living allowance, pension credit, council tax benefit, child tax benefit or income-based jobseeker's allowance – are entitled to extra help with their energy bills, many other households across the UK could also qualify for some assistance.

There are four different organisations across the UK. Both the range of help and the eligibility criteria differ between countries: with some schemes you need to be in receipt of certain benefits, while others are available to anyone over a particular age. Full details of what's on offer and how to apply can be found via the following links:

- England: Warm Front: *www.warmfront.co.uk* or phone 0800 316 2805
- Wales: Home Energy Efficiency Scheme: *www.heeswales.co.uk* or phone 0800 316 2815

- Scotland: Warm Deal and the Central Heating Programme: *www.communitiesscotland.gov.uk/ stellent/groups/public/documents/webpages/ cs_006584.hcsp* or phone 0800 316 1653
- Northern Ireland: Warm Homes: *www.eaga.com/government_contracts/ warmerhomes.htm* or phone 0800 181667.

Winter fuel payment

The government also offers a tax-free annual payment to households that include someone aged over 60 or over 80 (as at the qualifying date, usually the third week of September). For Winter 2008/9 this was worth £125 or £250 for those over 60, and either £200 or £400 for those aged over 80.

If the qualifying adult is already in receipt of benefits, such as the state pension or pension credit, they should receive the winter fuel payment automatically. However, it is possible to claim a payment until the end of March after the relevant winter.

As the state pension age for women rises from 60 to 65 between 2010 and 2020, so the qualifying age for the Winter Fuel Payment will also go up in tandem. Therefore, from winter 2010/11 onwards, both men and women will have to have reached the women's state pension age by the end of the September qualifying week to be entitled to the Winter Fuel Payment.

Find out more from: *www.thepensionservice.gov.uk/ winterfuel* or by phoning 0845 915 1515.

Home Improvement Agencies

Additional practical help may be available from Home Improvement Agencies (HIAs) across the UK. These are not-for-profit organisations that have been set up to repair, improve or adapt the properties of older, disabled and vulnerable homeowners or private tenants.

HIAs can offer advice about what work might be needed, identify financial assistance you might be entitled to, recommend contractors and help oversee the work. The initial advice is free; there may be a cost for further help but this can often be covered by the grant for the work itself. Find out more from the relevant body for England, Wales, Scotland or Northern Ireland:

- England: *www.foundations.uk.com* or phone 01457 891909
- Wales: Care & Repair Cymru: *www.careandrepair.org.uk* or phone 029 2057 6286
- Scotland: Care & Repair Forum Scotland: *www.careandrepairscotland.co.uk* or phone 0141 221 9879
- Northern Ireland: Fold Housing Association: *www.foldgroup.co.uk* or phone 028 9042 8314.

Industry

Each energy supplier has a responsibility to put in place measures to help 'vulnerable' customers.

In practice, this means that if you are receiving benefits such as disability living allowance, pension credit, council tax benefit, child tax benefit or income-based jobseeker's allowance, or, if you are over pensionable age, you could qualify for a reduced (or 'social') tariff, or be eligible for a rebate or an additional grant to boost your home's energy efficiency.

To find out more, contact the free industry-funded Home Heat Helpline, which offers advice to any customer who is struggling with their bills, whoever their supplier is. Go to: *www.homeheathelpline.org.uk* or phone 0800 336699.

Water

Water is a monopoly service so you cannot switch provider. However, you can explore whether you would save money by getting a meter. If so, reducing your actual water consumption could result in real savings.

Estimates suggest a single person living alone in an average property could save around £100 by switching. Households with higher than average bills may also benefit. The online calculator on the Consumer Council for Water's website can show if a meter might make sense for you: *www.ccwater.org.uk.*

Suppliers install meters for free and, in most cases, you can revert to non-metered status within twelve months if your bills rise.

Those who already have a meter can cut their bills by using less water: the Consumer Council for Water suggests an average metered household

could save around £25 a year by reducing its
water waste by just 10%.

Top tips

1. Take showers instead of baths, and use a
   shower timer to try to keep your showers
   short.

2. Put a 'hippo' or other water displacement
   device in your toilet cistern to reduce the
   amount of water used for each flush. Most
   water companies provide these for free.

3. Turning off the tap while cleaning your teeth or
   shaving can save approximately five litres a
   minute.

4. Fix any dripping taps – just two drips a
   second add up to about 26 litres of wasted
   water a day.

5. Only run your dishwasher or washing machine
   when it's full: 'half-loads' use more than half
   the amount of water and energy as a full load.

6. Use the cold water that comes through the
   tap before it runs hot to water plants or fill the
   kettle.

7. Make sure any new toilet is a low-flush or
   dual-flush model. Similarly, try to choose a
   washing machine or dishwasher that uses
   less than 50 litres per wash.

8. In the garden, consider installing a water
   butt and using a watering can rather than a
   hosepipe. If you must use a hose or a
   sprinkler, water early in the morning or late
   in the evening when less water will
   evaporate.

9. Use a bucket (ideally filled from the water butt) to wash the car instead of a running hose.

10. Check that you are being billed correctly: if you have a septic tank or cesspit, you should not be charged for wastewater. In the same way, if all the rainwater from your roof and surrounding surfaces drains to a soakaway or directly into a stream, river or canal, you are entitled to a refund of surface water drainage charges.

Find more advice at:

- *www.environment-agency.gov.uk/savewater*
- *www.ofwat.gov.uk/consumerissues*
- *www.waterwise.org.uk*
- *www.ccwater.org.uk.*

Extra help

Metered households that are deemed to be 'vulnerable' can have their water bills capped at the level of the average bill in their local area. To qualify, someone in the household needs to be in receipt of one of seven benefits and they must have three or more children under the age of 19 or have a qualifying medical condition that requires additional use of water.

Find out more from your water company or Ofwat at: *www.ofwat.gov.uk/consumerissues.*

Telephone/mobile/broadband

Just as you can move energy supplier, so you can switch your home telephone, mobile or broadband provider. Many companies offer special deals if you sign up for a 'bundle', which includes two or all three of the above services. Most of the price comparison websites mentioned below will let you search for single service or bundled deals.

Home telephone

A number of companies offer a variety of home phone services in the UK including BT, cable firm Virgin Media, high street names such as the Post Office and Tesco as well as several smaller operators.

You have a number of options: you can switch to a cable provider such as Virgin Media (formerly NTL Telewest); you can continue to pay line rental to BT but make some or all of your calls with rival companies; or you can opt for a new total residential phone service through Wholesale Line Rental (WLR), which means you no longer pay line rental to BT.

In most cases, you should be able to keep your phone number, whether you are switching your entire service or just using a second supplier for your calls. But if you switch to a cable provider, in certain circumstances you may need to change your number.

As with energy deals, comparison websites can help you work out which deal might suit your circumstances. You need to provide your postcode and answer some questions about your call usage. The site will then rank the different offers and let you apply.

The telecoms regulator Ofcom has recently launched an accreditation scheme for telecoms comparison websites. At the time of writing, only two companies have been accredited: Simplify Digital: *www.simplifydigital.co.uk* and BroadbandChoices: *www.broadbandchoices.co.uk.*

Other companies that let you compare different home phone providers (but that have not yet been accredited by Ofcom) include:

- uSwitch: *www.uswitch.com*
- Simply Switch: *www.simplyswitch.com*
- Landline Saver: *www.landlinesaver.co.uk.*

You can choose between many different telephone packages. Some allow unlimited national or local calls at certain times of the day in return for a monthly fixed fee. Others offer a cheaper line rental but more expensive call charges, which may be suitable for people who don't make many calls.

So, as well as comparing the basics, such as line rental and the cost of calls, you should think about the way you use the phone. What kind of calls do you make – i.e. local, national, international and mobile – when do you make calls and how many calls do you make? Are calls charged by the second, the minute or part-minute? Are there minimum call charges?

If you are considering using a separate company to make your calls, are you happy to have two contracts and receive two bills?

Remember, not all sites offer services from all providers, so you might want to put your details into a couple of different ones.

You can compare information about different telecoms providers' quality of service at: *www.topcomm.org.uk*. And you can find out more about switching from Ofcom itself at: *www.ofcom.org.uk/consumeradvice.*

Mobile

There are five mobile network operating companies in the UK – Vodafone, O2, Orange, T-Mobile and 3. In addition, there are many other 'virtual network operators' such as Tesco, Virgin Mobile and BT mobile, which use one of these five networks to provide a service under their own brand name.

They offer 'pre-pay' deals where you buy credits for the phone before you can make calls or send texts, and contract deals where you are billed, usually monthly, for the calls and texts you have made.

With a pre-pay deal, you generally have to buy your own handset, and calls and texts tend to be more expensive, but you only pay when you use the phone, and you can end the service at any time. Conversely, with a monthly contract, you will be offered a choice of free handset and can choose between a variety of different price packages. Calls, texts and accessing the internet should be cheaper but you do have to commit yourself to a fixed-term contract of typically 12 or 18 months.

What you can do with your phone (and what it will cost you) will depend on your particular handset, your network provider and your individual tariff. If you want to be able to surf the web on your mobile, then you probably need a '3G' or 'third generation' phone and service.

Consider which network the friends and family you speak to most regularly use; calls between the same network are often cheaper.

All mobile phone companies are required to transfer a customer's number within two business days. You have the right to take your number with you when you move to a new mobile operator, although you may be charged a fee to do so. Providers may not unlock your number until the end of your contract. In any case, you would still have to pay the monthly charges due under the contract.

Once you do decide to move, again, price comparison websites can help you choose between different deals.

At the time of writing, Ofcom has only accredited two telecoms price comparison websites: Simplify Digital: *www.simplifydigital.co.uk* and: *www.broadbandchoices.co.uk,* neither of which currently lets you compare mobile deals.

Sites that do (but that have not yet been accredited by Ofcom) include:

- uSwitch: *www.uswitch.com*
- Simply Switch: *www.simplyswitch.com*

- Moneysupermarket: *www.moneysupermarket.com*
- The Carphone Warehouse: *www.carphonewarehouse.com*
- Phones4u: *www.phones4u.co.uk.*

Factors to compare include the cost of line rental; the number of free minutes and texts, and the cost of each if you exceed your monthly allowance; the cost of making and receiving calls abroad; the features and cost of the available handsets; the cost of accessing and downloading material from the internet; and the cost of retrieving messages from the voicemail service.

In the same way, you can also use the websites to help you compare deals for mobile broadband.

But remember that not all sites let you compare all available deals, so put your details into a few.

If you are abroad for an extended period, you may wish to buy a 'SIM' card linked to a local mobile network as this can work out considerably cheaper than using your UK phone. You can buy them at airports or when you arrive at your destination.

In addition, you can compare the geographic network performance and voice call quality of each of the GSM mobile network operators: O2, Orange, Vodafone and T-Mobile at: *www.topnetuk.com.* Find out more about switching mobile contracts at: *www.ofcom.org.uk/consumeradvice/mobile.*

Broadband

The rapid improvement in broadband technology mean that better, faster and more reliable broadband should be increasingly available.

People living in rural or isolated areas may find they cannot access traditional broadband services. However, many local communities have banded together to make it economically viable. Find out more at: www.defra.gov.uk/rural/broadband.

However, despite the theoretical advances, many customers find the speed and reliability of their service falls well short of the promised standards.

In December 2008 the telecoms regulator Ofcom launched a code of practice to try to ensure that consumers get more accurate information about broadband speeds. You can find out how to complain about your internet service provider at: *www.ofcom.org.uk/complain/internet.*

Of course, if you're still unhappy, you can switch provider altogether.

You will normally need to wait until the end of your present contract before you can switch – or face paying a cancellation charge.

In order to switch broadband contracts, you need to get something called a MAC (Migration Action Code) from your present provider. This must be provided within five working days. Once you have this code, you can start searching for a new deal.

 If you are just switching from one (non-cable) broadband service provider to another, you should be able to keep your home telephone number.

As before, internet comparison websites can help you rank different offers once you've provided your postcode. However, unlike energy switching sites, with broadband you make the actual application via the new provider's own website.

At the time of writing, Ofcom has only accredited two telecoms price comparison websites: Simplify Digital: *www.simplifydigital.co.uk* and Broadband Choices: *www.broadbandchoices.co.uk.*

Other sites that will let you compare broadband deals (but that have not yet been accredited by Ofcom) include:

- uSwitch: *www.uswitch.com*
- Simply Switch: *www.simplyswitch.com*
- Moneysupermarket: *www.moneysupermarket.com*
- Think Broadband: *www.thinkbroadband.com*
- Broadband Genie: *www.broadbandgenie.co.uk.*

 Remember not all sites offer services from all providers, so you might want to put your details into a couple of different ones.

Factors to consider include the cost, the advertised speed, whether there are any restrictions on usage, the length of the contract, whether you will need to buy any additional equipment and whether you can add extra computers to the broadband connection.

Don't just be led by price: make sure you are comparing like with like in terms of promised speed and data restrictions.

If your email address is provided by your current internet service supplier, you may lose it when you switch supplier. Some providers offer a three-month grace period to allow you time to transfer your contacts etc. Once your new account is up and running, you should be able to set up a redirect from your old address to the new one. In the meantime, it can be useful to have a free internet email account (such as Hotmail, Yahoo! or gmail) during the switchover since you can access such accounts from any computer.

Find out more at: *www.ofcom.org.uk/consumeradvice/internet.*

Summary

Whether you want to compare prices, switch energy suppliers or telecoms providers, the internet can be an invaluable tool.

Even if you can't or don't want to switch, you can also find an enormous amount of helpful advice about how to reduce your consumption and save yourself money in the process.

7

Taxes and benefits

As far as both taxes and benefits are concerned, the internet offers an incredible amount of information and advice.

But it's possible to do much more. You can use your computer to access a huge variety of government services from the comfort of your keyboard – from applying for incapacity benefit to requesting a state pension forecast to submitting your tax return.

The Directgov website has an excellent summary of all the ways you can engage with government online. Find it at: *www.direct.gov.uk/en/ Dio/1/DoItOnline.*

Personal tax

Self Assessment

If you are one of the millions of UK citizens who has to make a Self Assessment (SA) tax return every year (perhaps because you are self-employed or you have multiple sources of income), the government would very much like you to submit that return via the internet.

Tax returns (or a notice to fill one in if you file online) are usually sent out in April each year. If you have not received anything but think you may need to submit one, contact your tax office, ring the Self Assessment Helpline on 0845 900 0444 or go to: www.hmrc.gov.uk/sa. If you do receive a tax return, you must complete it, even if you are taxed through PAYE and therefore do not believe you have any extra to pay.

In recent years HM Revenue & Customs (HMRC) has taken various steps to encourage online filing, including bringing forward the deadline for paper returns. It highlights a number of other advantages for those who go down this route:

1. The amount of tax you owe is worked out automatically as you input your details, meaning you find out how much you need to pay (or claim back) instantly.

You can also file in stages: input some details, save the form and return to it later.

2. You get an immediate online acknowledgement that HMRC has received your completed form. Receipts are not provided if you post the paper form or deliver it in person to your local tax office.

3. Online returns are processed more quickly than paper returns, meaning you should receive any money due to you more swiftly as well.

4. You can access the online service 24 hours a day, so you can submit your return whenever it suits you.

HMRC recommends that people with PCs who wish to access the SA online system use Microsoft Internet Explorer version 5.0 or later, and those with Macs use Safari version 2.0.4 or later. Users of other web browsers (such as Mozilla Firefox) may not have full access to the site.

5. You can also see your latest statement of account and check what you owe/are owed, as well as see details of your payment history.

You can either use HMRC's free system to file your tax return online or use commercially available software, some of which is also freely available. Rather oddly, HMRC's system does not support all the Self Assessment supplementary pages but the commercial software does. Find out more about third-party filing systems on HMRC's website at: www.hmrc.gov.uk/efiling/sa_efiling/ soft_dev.htm#individuals.

Registration

In order to use Self Assessment online, you need to register via the HMRC website at: *online.hmrc.gov.uk/registration.*

When you register you will be asked for your Unique Taxpayer Reference (UTR) number, which is printed at the top of your tax return. This is made up of ten numbers followed by the letter K – e.g. 1234567890K. You will also need either your postcode or National Insurance (NI) number.

You then select 'register' in the New User section and select 'Self Assessment Online' as the service you wish to access. On-screen instructions will guide you through the next steps, including accepting the terms and conditions of usage and creating your password.

The Government Gateway – the central registration service for all online government services for individuals – will then send you a User ID and Activation PIN (personal identification number) within seven days.

You have 28 days in which to use your Activation PIN before it expires.

Once you have these, return to: *www.hmrc.gov.uk/ sa,* select 'Log in to file your tax return online' and log in using your User ID and the password you set up earlier. Follow the instructions.

Once you have activated your account, you can use the same User ID and password to sign up to access other online government services for individuals, including Child Benefit Online or VAT Online.

Find out more at: *www.hmrc.gov.uk/sa/ file-online.htm* or contact HMRC's dedicated Online Services Helpdesk on 0845 605 5999. Alternatively, you can email: *helpdesk@ir-efile.gov.uk.*

Settling up

Once you have submitted your form, you are then responsible for ensuring you pay any tax due by 31 January – or face a fine of £100 (although the penalty cannot be more than the tax you owe, so if you owe less than £100 you should not be fined).

Find out more about deadlines and penalties at: www.hmrc.gov.uk/sa/dead-pen.htm.

HMRC recommends that customers pay electronically. You can do this by setting up a direct debit (if you have registered for SA online) or via internet or telephone banking if not.

To pay electronically, you will need to give your bank or building society HMRC's bank account details. HMRC has two accounts that accept payments; your payment reminder should tell you which one to use.

Accounts office	Sort code	Account number	Account name
Cumbernauld	10 51 67	23444401	AO Cumbernauld
Shipley	10 50 41	23456000	AO Shipley

Make sure you quote your Unique Taxpayer Reference (UTR) when making the payment.

Alternatively, you can pay your tax over the phone or via internet banking by using a debit card (but not a credit card). Find out more at: *www.billpayment.co.uk/hmrc.*

More from HMRC

The HMRC website has a great deal of other useful information and advice about all aspects of taxation including tax allowances, income tax, national insurance (NI), capital gains tax (CGT), child and family tax credits and inheritance tax (IHT).

Find out more from: www.hmrc.gov.uk. Find details of HMRC's extensive range of helplines at: www.hmrc.gov.uk/ menus.contactus.shtml.

As we discussed in Chapter 3, if you are a non-taxpayer you can register to get the interest you receive on any savings account 'gross' – i.e. without tax deducted. You need to fill out HMRC form R85 for each institution where you hold an account you wish to register, and then give it to the relevant bank or building society. If you have a joint account and only one of you is a taxpayer, you can arrange to have half the interest paid gross.

Use HMRC's online calculator to help you work out if you are entitled to get interest paid gross at: www.hmrc.gov.uk/calcs/ r85.htm.

If you do qualify, you can find the form at: *www.hmrc.gov.uk/forms/r85.pdf* and the guidance notes at: *www.hmrc.gov.uk/helpsheets/ r85-helpsheet.pdf* or phone 0845 980 0645 for assistance.

If you have paid too much tax on your bank or building society interest in the past, you can reclaim it by filling out HMRC form R40. You can backdate the claim to cover the previous six tax years.

You can find the form at: *www.hmrc.gov.uk/forms/r40.pdf* and the guidance notes at: *www.hmrc.gov.uk/forms/r40notes.pdf.*

For other information about reclaiming tax in other circumstances, visit: *www.hmrc.gov.uk/incometax/refund-reclaim.htm.*

Council tax

The level of your council tax (or rates in Northern Ireland) is set by your local council.

For general information about council tax, visit: www.direct.gov.uk/en/HomeAndCommunity/YourlocalcouncilandCouncilTax/.

The internet can help you check that your property is in the correct council tax band, and find out whether you are eligible for any discounts, exemptions or financial help.

To check your council tax band, you need to go to the website of the Valuation Office Agency, part of HMRC: *www.voa.gov.uk/news/information/your_council_tax_band.htm.*

You can use the search function to discover what band your property is in and, if you think it is wrong (if, for instance, other similar properties in the same street are in a lower band), you can ask for it to be reviewed by contacting your local valuation office.

You may discover that your property is in a lower band than it should be, which would mean your council tax would go up.

Taxpayers with enquiries about council tax bands for Scottish properties should contact the Scottish Assessors at: *www.saa.gov.uk.*

Ratepayers with enquiries about Northern Irish properties should contact Land and Property Services Northern Ireland at: *www.lpsni.gov.uk.*

Paying less council tax

You may be able to pay less council tax if your property is empty; if only one adult lives there; or if you are disabled, a student or a nurse. If you are on a low income, you may qualify for Council Tax Benefit.

Contact your local council for more information about reductions, exemptions and benefit eligibility. See below for further details about claiming benefits in general.

General help with tax from other sources

The government information website Directgov has admirably clear information about all aspects of tax at: *www.direct.gov.uk/en/ MoneyTaxAndBenefits/Taxes.*

In addition, two independent organisations may also be useful.

Tax Aid is a charity that offers free, independent and confidential advice to anyone who has a tax problem but cannot afford to pay an accountant or tax adviser. It runs a national helpline and offers face-to-face advice services in London, Birmingham and Manchester.

You can phone the helpline on 0845 120 3779 between 10am and 12 midday, Mondays to Thursdays or go to: *www.taxaid.org.uk.*

Another charity, Tax Help for Older People (TOP), offers free and confidential advice to pensioners with a household income of less than £15,000 per year.

More than 500 TOP tax advisers run surgeries at more than 270 venues across the UK and can provide home visits if required. Simple advice can be provided over the phone.

To find out more, phone 0845 601 3321, email: *taxvol@taxvol.org.uk or go to: www.taxvol.org.uk.*

Benefits

As with tax, you can find a great deal of information about benefits online.

It is possible to split the range of benefits available in the UK into four categories: those for people of working age, those for people who have retired or are planning to retire, those for families and children and those for disabled people and their carers.

A number of government agencies and departments share responsibility for these different areas – such as The Pension Service, Jobcentre Plus, HMRC – and it can be very confusing to identify the right place to go to for specific benefits. The internet can be invaluable in tracking down the answers you need.

General guidance

You can find an excellent overview of all the benefits that are available, who administers them – and how to apply for them – on the government's information website Directgov. Go to: *www.direct.gov.uk/en/MoneyTaxAndBenefits* and click on 'Benefits and Financial Support'.

The main contacts are as follows:

- The Department for Work and Pensions (DWP): *www.dwp.gov.uk*
- The Pension Service: *www.thepensionservice.gov.uk*
- Service Personnel and Veterans Agency: *www.veterans-uk.info*
- Disability and Carers Service: *www.dwp.gov.uk/lifeevent/benefits/dcs*
- obcentre Plus: *www.jobcentreplus.gov.uk*
- HM Revenue & Customs (HMRC): *www.hmrc.gov.uk*
- Child Support Agency (CSA): *www.csa.gov.uk.*

The DWP website has a very useful list of contacts for different benefits including more detailed web addresses and helpline telephone numbers: *www.dwp.gov.uk/contact.*

The Directgov website also has a useful calculator to help you work out which benefits you might be entitled to: *www.campaigns.direct.gov.uk/benefitsadviser.*

You can also check your entitlement to benefits on an independent (but well-respected) website called: *www.entitled2.co.uk.*

Citizens Advice's online Advice Guide is another excellent tool. Find it at: *www.adviceguide.org.uk.* If you need face-to-face advice, search for your local Citizens Advice Bureau at: *www.citizensadvice.org.uk.*

What can you actually do online?

As we said at the beginning of the chapter, you can do more than find generic guidance about what help is available. You can find detailed information about the help available and find claim forms for many benefits on the relevant department's website.

In addition, you can actually apply for a number of benefits online including Income Support, Jobseeker's Allowance, Disability Living Allowance, Employment and Support Allowance and Incapacity Benefit.

Go to 'Services and Benefits online' on the DWP website at: *www.dwp.gov.uk/eservice.*

The site has been configured for PC users running browsers including Internet Explorer version 6.0, Netscape version 7.2, and Firefox version1.0.3, but, at the time of writing, the service is not available to Mac users. You do not need an email address.

If you have already registered via the Government Gateway (see earlier section about registering to file your tax return online), you can use your existing User ID and password to access the service. If not, you can select the 'new user' option.

There is a dedicated Helpdesk available on 0845 601 8040 (or +44 191 218 7777 for Pension Service customers calling from an international number).

Extra assistance for pensioners

As well as the usual information about how to apply for the different benefits available, there are several other valuable online services for pensioners, or those approaching pensionable age.

Perhaps the most useful is the ability to request a State Pension forecast. As the name suggests, this provides an estimate of the amount of State Pension you might be entitled to in the future.

To apply for an instant forecast, go to: *www.thepensionservice.gov.uk/state-pension/forecast.*

In order to be able to use the online service, you must live in the UK, be more than four months away from State Pension age and not be widowed or someone whose civil partner has died.

If you have not already registered, select the option for new users and you will be taken to a registration window.

You can get further assistance from the e-services helpdesk on 0845 601 8040 or the State Pension Forecasting Team on 0845 3000 168.

Another helpful tool is the *State Pension Age calculator*, which works out when you will become eligible for the State Pension.

The calculator is necessary because the State Pension age is changing. From 6 April 2020 it will be 65 for both men and women. Therefore, women's State Pension age will gradually increase from 2010 onwards. Women born on or before 5 April 1950 will not be affected and will still be able to claim their State Pension at 60, but all those with later birthdays will have to wait longer before they qualify.

In addition, the State Pension age for both men and women will rise from 65 to 68 between 2024 and 2046, with each change phased in over two consecutive years in each decade.

Find your State Pension age by entering your gender and date of birth at: *www.thepensionservice.gov.uk/state-pension/age-calculator.asp.*

Another potentially useful (and free) online facility is the Pensions Tracing Service, which tries to track down details of either occupational or personal pension schemes with which you've lost touch.

You are asked to provide as much information as possible about the employer or pension scheme in question and the relevant dates when you were a member. It then runs those details through its database and, if there is a successful match, you are given the contact details for the relevant scheme.

The Tracing Service cannot tell you if you are entitled to any payments from the scheme – it's up to you to contact the scheme administrator to find out more.

Apply at: *www.thepensionservice.gov.uk* or phone 0845 600 2537.

More help

I've already mentioned the Directgov and Citizens Advice websites as excellent general resources.

The Community Legal Advice website also has useful information about your legal rights to welfare and how to challenge benefit decisions at: *www.communitylegaladvice.org.uk* or call 0845 345 4 345. Your local council may have a welfare rights team – look on its website or in the phone book.

In addition, the following organisations' websites and/or helplines have lots of specific information about their relevant areas.

Working age/families and children

- Working Families: *www.workingfamilies.org.uk* or phone 0800 013 0313
- Gingerbread/National Council for One Parent Families: *www.gingerbread.org.uk/* and *www.oneparentfamilies.org.uk* or phone 0800 018 5026
- Child Poverty Action Group: *www.cpag.org.uk.*

Pensioners

- Pensions Advisory Service: *www.pensionsadvisoryservice.org.uk* or phone 0845 601 2923
- Age Concern: *www.ageconcern.org.uk* or phone 0800 00 99 66
- Help the Aged: *www.helptheaged.org.uk* or phone 0008 800 6565
- National Pensioners Convention: *www.npcuk.org.*

Disability/carers

- Disability Alliance: *www.disabilityalliance.org*
- Dial UK: *www.dialuk.info*
- Disability Law Service: *www.dls.org.uk* or phone 020 7791 9800
- Focus on Disability: *www.focusondisability.org.uk*
- Advice Now: *www.advicenow.org.uk*
- Carers UK: *www.carersuk.org* or phone 0808 808 7777
- The Princess Royal Trust for Carers: *www.carers.org* or email: help@carers.org
- Crossroads: *www.crossroads.org.uk* or phone 0845 450 0350.

Debt

The following organisations can offer free and confidential advice about living on a low income and dealing with debts:

- Consumer Credit Counselling Service: *www.cccs.co.uk* or phone 0800 138 1111
- National Debtline: *www.nationaldebtline.co.uk* or freephone 0800 808 4000.

Summary

As we have seen, the internet can supply an enormous amount of information and advice about tax and benefits through countless websites, both official and unofficial.

But it can do much more than that. It can also be an active and flexible tool, which lets you engage directly with key government services at a time and in a place that suits you, whether that's during standard office hours, on Christmas Day or in the middle of the night.

It's just further proof of how revolutionary – and liberating – managing your money online can be.

8

Buying and selling online

The internet has profoundly revolutionised the way we shop. It's now possible to compare prices of hundreds of thousands of items from tens of thousands of suppliers all over the world without stepping outside your front door.

The same technology that has empowered buyers can also be exploited by those who want to sell their own goods, via online auction sites such as eBay, and other trading sites such as Amazon Marketplace and Loot.com.

However, as we've already discussed, the nature of the web means you cannot always be sure exactly with whom you are dealing – or where in the world they are – so you need to keep your wits about you to make sure you buy and sell online safely.

Buying online

You can buy anything on the internet that you can buy on the high street and much more besides. All major retailers now have an online presence but you will also find thousands of companies that save money by not having expensive premises open to the public, and that pass those savings on to their customers.

You can buy your groceries online; you can find specialist dealers online; you can commission bespoke goods online and, crucially, you can shop around to ensure you pay a competitive price on anything from books, CDs and DVDs to stereos, fridges and even cars.

In fact, there are many websites designed to help you quickly and easily search various retailers' sites for the item you want. Well-known companies operating in this area include:

- Pricerunner: *www.pricerunner.co.uk*
- Kelkoo: *www.kelkoo.co.uk*
- Twenga: *www.twenga.co.uk*
- Shopping: *www.shopping.com/uk.*

tip

Make sure you are comparing like with like – i.e. that the price you see takes into account all taxes and delivery costs as these can vary enormously. If you buy certain expensive goods from abroad you may also have to pay customs duty. Find out more at: www.hmrc.gov.uk.

Once you have found an item you want, take the time to find out more about the retailer before going ahead. After all, you wouldn't hand over cash to someone you didn't trust – and nor should you give your credit card details to any company that you don't feel confident about.

Don't assume that a company is based in the UK just because it ends in '.co.uk'. Make sure you have a full address – not just a PO Box number – and preferably a landline contact telephone number. If in doubt, ring the company or send an email before you buy anything.

In Chapter 2 we talked about making sure a website is secure before giving it our confidential data. Look out for the letters 'https' (where the 's' stands for secure) in front of the web address, and a small padlock. A legitimate site should also offer information about its privacy policy – such as whether it guarantees not to sell your personal details to third parties.

Most online retailers will ask you to register your email address and a unique password to set up an account. There is advice about creating 'strong' passwords in Chapter 2.

You may want to open a separate free email account to use for online shopping, but make sure you remember which one you pick as you will need it to access the site in the future. Order confirmations and delivery information will also be sent to it. You can ask for a reminder to be sent to your registered email address if you forget your password.

The advantage of registering is that the site can then remember your credit card and address details. In some cases, sites will also store the addresses of people to whom you regularly send things.

Beware: some websites will only deliver to the registered address of the credit card holder to help combat fraud.

Many online retailers use a third-party payments system to process credit and debit card payments on their behalf, such as PayPal, World Pay or Nochex. In such cases, you provide your details to the payment company itself rather than the retailer. There's more about PayPal in the eBay section to follow.

Some sellers will accept cheque payments but, if the goods you are buying cost between £100 and £30,000, you should ideally pay by credit card as this will give you extra consumer protection if the items are faulty or do not arrive. This protection can even apply (in some cases) to goods bought from foreign sites.

In fact, anyone buying an item over the internet from a UK company should have more protection than if they bought the same item in a UK shop, the most important aspect of which is the right to a 'cooling off' period. This gives you the right to cancel your purchase within seven working days, unless the goods are made to order or are perishable.

Some firms insist that you pay the cost of returning any unwanted items.

In addition, if you haven't received the goods within thirty days – or a longer period if agreed at the outset – you have the right to cancel the order and get a refund or a replacement.

If the goods are damaged or substantially different from the online description, again, you can ask for your money back. But if there is a delay before you realise the goods are faulty, you may only be entitled to have the goods replaced or repaired.

If the goods cannot be replaced or repaired, you will be entitled to a refund or the cost of buying the goods from another retailer.

Remember, these rights apply to goods bought from UK websites, and – in some circumstances – those based within the EU but not for sites based in other jurisdictions.

Find out more about your rights when shopping online by contacting Consumer Direct at: *www.consumerdirect.gov.uk* or by phoning 08454 04 05 06.

eBay

eBay is primarily an online auction site. Sellers list items for a set period of time and invite bids. In response, buyers make offers, and the highest bidder at the close of the auction gets the goods. The system can let you know when someone bids more than you, or even keep bidding on your behalf up to a pre-set limit. Beware, the bids tend to rise sharply towards the close of the auction.

Many eBay sellers also offer goods for sale at a fixed 'buy it now' price.

You need to register to be able to buy or bid for something on eBay. Registration is free; you are asked to provide an email address and credit card details to validate your identity but you will not be charged. You then choose a username by which you will be known to buyers and sellers on the site.

When you buy something via an auction site such as eBay (or with any of the other sites where private individuals can offer their goods), your contract is with the individual seller, and not with eBay itself. This matters because when you buy from a private seller you have fewer rights than if you buy from a business.

 By placing a bid on eBay you are entering into an agreement, meaning if you are successful, you cannot change your mind and decide you no longer want the item.

Before bidding, or buying anything, you should therefore read the item description very carefully. Does it say the goods are new? Is a particular brand specified? Is there a photo? Check what payment methods the seller accepts, what they charge for postage and their returns policy.

The other crucial thing to consider is the seller's positive feedback rating. Click on the seller's name to see detailed comments made by previous customers. Needless to say, think very carefully before buying something from a seller with a low score.

You should also be suspicious if an item is significantly cheaper than you would expect it to be, given the description. If in doubt, contact the seller directly to find out more.

Paying

Sellers can accept a range of payment options, but eBay prefers people to use its own online payment system, PayPal. Under this system, buyers make a payment to PayPal using their credit or debit card. PayPal then pays the seller without disclosing the buyer's financial details.

You can also transfer money from your bank account to your PayPal account and use the balance to pay for goods online.

PayPal also offers a dispute resolution service if you don't receive an item or if it is significantly different from the initial description. If PayPal finds in your favour, you could receive a full refund of the purchase price plus postage costs, although the process is not necessarily swift. Find out more at: *www.PayPal.co.uk.*

Whatever your experience, you are encouraged to leave feedback on the seller's profile to help inform future potential customers. Be aware – sellers can also leave feedback on buyers!

Find out more at: *www.eBay.co.uk.*

Buying from private individuals on other sites

As we will discuss shortly, there are many other sites where you can buy goods from private sellers.

Much of the advice for using eBay remains pertinent for purchases from these other websites.

1. Remember, you have fewer rights than if you buy from a business.

2. Find out as much as you can about the item and the seller before going ahead. Check the seller's reputation and read comments from previous customers.

3. Be suspicious if a deal seems too good to be true: a legitimate seller will not object to verifying information.

4. If you are buying an item costing between £100 and £30,000, consider using your credit card to give you extra consumer protection.

5. If you can't pay by credit card, or the amount is worth less than £100, try to use a third-party payment system such as PayPal, which offers a dispute resolution service.

6. If there is a problem, communicate with your seller. Most people are acting in good faith – so give them the opportunity to put a mistake right.

7. If in the end you are still unhappy, you can leave negative feedback – but make sure what you say is factually accurate and not just abusive.

Selling online

If you can buy online, it means someone else is selling online, and that someone could be you.

In the past, people keen to get rid of old clothes and books or unwanted gifts may have tried to sell them at a car boot sale, put an advert in their local paper or even just given them to a charity shop.

Thanks to the internet, there's another option: sell your unwanted goods online and take advantage of an enormous potential audience that might be interested in buying them.

There are a number of sites where you can sell your stuff. eBay is obviously the best known, but there are others:

- Amazon Marketplace: *www.amazon.co.uk/ marketplace*
- Play Trade: *www.play.com/playtrade*
- Loot: *www.loot.com*
- Gumtree: *www.gumtree.com*
- Craig's list: *www.geo.craigslist.org/iso/gb*.

Money, money, money

One of the main advantages of selling your goods via a large site like eBay or Amazon is that you can benefit from their existing payments system.

As we've already discussed, eBay prefers buyers and sellers to use PayPal, although you can choose to accept other payment methods if you wish – with the exception of money transfers, which are banned because of their lack of traceability.

But with Amazon Marketplace, for instance, customers buying an item from a third-party 'Marketplace' seller pay Amazon in exactly the same way as if they'd bought the goods from the main company. The seller is only notified about the sale once the payment has been safely received, thus reducing the risk of non-payment. Amazon then transfers the money minus the relevant fee into the seller's bank account.

However, with some other sites, it's up to you to decide what payment methods you will accept. If you decide to take cheques, you should wait until the cheque has cleared in your bank account before dispatching the goods, having made this clear to your buyer at the outset.

For more about cheque clearance, go to: www.apacs.org.uk/payment_options/2-4-6.html.

Watch out for a common scam whereby you sell an item for one price – say £50 – but your buyer sends you a cheque for a larger amount – such as £100 – and requests that you send back a cheque for the difference. Typically their cheque will later bounce, leaving you out of pocket to the tune of the original £50 plus the extra £50 = £100. If someone tries to get you to accept a larger cheque as payment, refuse it – and consider cancelling the sale altogether.

Personal touch

As a private seller, you are not bound by the distance selling regulations we discussed in the section on buying. However, items you sell should be as you describe them and, in essence, you should treat customers as you would wish to be treated yourself.

Here are some more general tips about selling safely online:

1. Register with your chosen site; choose a username and password. You may wish to use a pseudonym as your username rather

than your real name or email address to help protect your privacy.

2. Make sure you understand if – and if so what – you will be charged for a) listing items and b) selling items on the site. How is the fee levied? Is it deducted from the purchase price before you receive it? Or will you be billed monthly for all fees incurred?

3. Find out what other people are charging for similar versions of your item. Depending on the pricing structure of the site in question, you may need to include the cost of postage in the price you set – especially if you decide you will dispatch goods internationally.

4. Be honest and accurate in your description – include as many details as you can, such as make, model, colour, dimensions etc. Post a photograph if you can. And don't be tempted to overstate the condition as you are only likely to annoy your buyer.

5. Check the site or your email account regularly – it is your responsibility to acknowledge and process orders when they arrive. Use clean packaging materials and dispatch the goods promptly. Wrap fragile items very carefully. Keep your buyer informed about the progress of their order. Remember, most systems invite buyers to rank the seller's performance, so make sure you provide the best service you can.

6. Get a proof of postage receipt from the Post Office when you send your items and keep this safe in case of any disputes with your buyer. However, proof of postage does not

allow you to trace a parcel, so you may wish to pay extra to send valuable items by recorded delivery. You could make a virtue of this and highlight it in your listing – but you may also need to increase your prices to cover the cost.

7. If a buyer says they have not received an item, you have to decide how to respond. Check that you have sent the item to the correct address. Royal Mail does not consider an item posted first class to be missing for 15 working days or 10 working days for Special Delivery items, so you may need to ask your buyer to be patient. Suggest they contact their local sorting office in case the parcel is waiting for collection there. Depending on which postal service you have used, you may be entitled to compensation from Royal Mail – if you have proof of postage. But regardless of formal compensation, you may need to refund your buyer – remember, they may leave negative feedback if you don't.

8. Similarly, if the item arrives damaged then you also need to decide whether to refund your buyer. Again, depending on which postal service you have used, you may be entitled to compensation from Royal Mail. Ask your buyer to keep the item and the packaging and, if possible, take photos of both to help support your claim. Find out more at: *www.royalmail.com/compensation*.

9. Be cautious about agreeing that a buyer can collect an item they have bought in person. It can save you the cost of packaging but you

may not want a stranger to come to your home. Consider meeting in a neutral environment like a cafe. You may want to ask them to sign something to say they have received the item.

10. If you are going on holiday – or simply won't have time to check your email or the website – consider delisting your items or activating 'holiday' settings if the site offers the feature. Otherwise you may find a lot of missed orders and negative feedback when you next log on.

Tax needn't be taxing

If you just use the internet to sell unwanted personal items on an ad hoc basis, you shouldn't need to worry about paying tax.

However, if you buy or make goods in order to sell them online, intending to make a profit, HM Revenue & Customs may consider you to be self-employed, in which case you may need to pay income tax and national insurance contributions. Registering as a business or 'pro' seller on any of these sites obviously suggests you are trading.

For further guidance, go to: *www.hmrc.gov.uk/ guidance/selling* or contact HMRC's newly self-employed helpline on 0845 915 4515.

Summary

The internet has changed the way we shop for ever, allowing us to find goods all over the world, and compare thousands of prices with just the click of a mouse.

The vast majority of businesses and sellers operating online are legitimate, and there are many bargains to be had. But that doesn't mean there are no risks to buying – or selling – online.

However, you can reduce those risks substantially by following the advice in this chapter. Make sure you understand what you're buying (or selling) and from (or to) whom and exactly what it will cost you, and the chances are you'll get yourself a good deal.

9
Having fun online

As we said at the beginning of the book, managing your money online could be just the start of a much bigger internet adventure. Once your computer is fully functioning and connected to the web, you can do so much more than check your bank statements and organise your insurance!

In addition to the following links, there are lots of useful contacts on the Directgov website at: *www.direct.gov.uk/en/Over50s.*

Here are just a few suggestions of online activities to get you started.

Keeping in touch
Email

When you set up your contract with your internet service provider (ISP) you will also have set up an email account, which you can use to keep in touch with people all over the world.

Some ISPs will let you have multiple email addresses through one account. Again, most of the major ISPs will let you access your account from anywhere in the word by using its own internet site (e.g. *www.aol.com*). Or you can set up entirely separate free 'webmail' accounts with other providers (e.g. Google, Yahoo! and Hotmail).

You may wish to have one email account for your banking and shopping and another for your friends and family to use. You can of course have as many email addresses as you like but you need to be able to remember your login details – and of course what you use each for – without having to compromise your security by writing details down.

Internet telephony

Email is not the only way your computer can keep you in contact with your friends and family. Using technology called 'voice over internet protocol', or VOIP, when your computer is online you can use it to make telephone calls, either to other users sitting at their computer or to landlines and mobiles all over the world.

Because such calls use the existing architecture of the internet to transmit your conversations, calls are either free or very cheap.

Not all VOIP systems are compatible; if the main reason for having VOIP is to speak to your grandchildren in Australia, make sure you use the same provider.

Whichever firm you sign up with, in most cases you need to download software to your machine and invest in either a headset with a microphone or a VOIP phone, both of which plug directly into your computer. If both ends are connected to a camera, you can also make video calls in this way.

You should be able to talk to compatible computers straight away; to talk to landlines or mobiles, you will probably have to buy phone credits. Here are a few of the many VOIP operators:

- Skype: *www.skype.com*
- Tesco Internet Phone: *www.tescointernetphone.com/*
- BT Broadband Talk: *www.bt.com/btbroadbandtalk*
- Gizmo: *gizmo5.com/pc*
- Vonage: *www.vonage.co.uk.*

Photo sharing

One of the best things about the internet is the ability to publish material that can then be accessed by people all over the world. Photo-sharing sites are a great example of this.

Once you register (usually a free process), you are allocated a certain amount of storage space, which you can then use to display your digital photographs online. This can also provide a useful way to back up some or all of your photos.

In most cases, you can determine your own privacy settings, meaning either anyone or only people you select can view your pictures. Many companies also let you order prints of photos you have uploaded. Here are some of the main photo-sharing sites:

- Flickr: *www.flickr.com*
- Picasa: *picasa.google.com*
- Photobox: *www.photobox.co.uk*
- Kodak: *www.kodakgallery.co.uk*

- Photobucket: *photobucket.com*
- Fotki: *www.fotki.com.*

Social networking sites/message boards

There are many websites designed to let people communicate with like-minded individuals. With social networking sites, registered users construct a personal profile that can be seen by fellow members and can be updated as the user wishes. Message boards are spaces on the internet where registered users can discuss various topics.

General
- Facebook: *www.facebook.com*
- Myspace: *www.myspace.com*
- Twitter: *www.twitter.com.*

For over 50s
- Age Concern Discuss:
  www.ageconcern.org.uk/discuss
- Saga Zone: *www.sagazone.co.uk*
- My Chums Club: *www.mychumsclub.com*
- Fifty Already: *www.fiftyalready.com*
- Fifty On: *www.fiftyon.co.uk*
- I don't feel fifty: *www.idf50.co.uk*
- Togs: *www.togs.org*
- 50 Connect: *www.50connect.co.uk.*

Dating

Dating agencies have also flourished on the internet. Some sites claim to have hundreds of thousands of registered members. All allow you to specify an age range for the people you would like to meet, but there are also dozens of companies that have been designed with the over 50s in mind.

Remember to use your judgement and common sense. Be careful before giving out your personal information, such as your address, phone number or email details. If you do arrange to meet, make sure you do so in a public place, and tell a friend where you are going to be. If you feel uncomfortable, make your excuses and leave.

You can find more useful advice from the Association of British Introduction Agencies at: *www.abia.org.uk* and *www.datesafely.co.uk.*

General sites

- Match.com: *www.uk.match.com*
- Dating Direct: *www.datingdirect.com*
- Friends Reunited Dating: *www.friendsreuniteddating.co.uk.*

For over 50s

- Senior Dating Group: *www.seniordatinggroup.co.uk*
- Friends Over Fifty: *www.friendsoverfifty.co.uk*
- Fifty Already: *www.fiftyalready.com.*

Other useful websites

The internet can be an incredibly helpful source of up-to-date information about all sorts of things, from recipes to train times, from theatre listings to the weather forecast, and so on.

Search engines

Type some key words (e.g. 'Bristol taxis', 'Christmas pudding recipe') into a search engine. The more specific your search terms, the more accurate the results will be.

There are many search engines, but here are some well-known ones:

- Google: *www.google.com*
- Ask: *www.ask.co.uk*
- Microsoft Live: *www.live.com*
- Yahoo!: *www.uk.yahoo.com.*

Weather

- The Met Office: *www.metoffice.gov.uk*
- BBC Weather: *www.bbc.co.uk/weather*
- The Weather Channel: *www.weather.co.uk.*

News

- BBC News: *news.bbc.co.uk*
- ITN News: *itn.co.uk*
- Channel 4 News: *www.channel4.com/news*
- Sky News: *news.sky.com/skynews*
- CNN: *www.cnn.com.*

Radio/TV

You can find listings online and also listen to and watch live programmes or catch up on earlier broadcasts.

- Radio Times: *www.radiotimes.com*
- TV Guide: *www.tvguide.co.uk*
- Information about digital radio: *www.digitalradionow.com*

- BBC iPlayer: *www.bbc.co.uk/iplayer*
- ITV: *www.itv.com*
- Channel 4: *www.channel4.com*
- Five: *www.five.tv.*

You can also download and subscribe to 'podcasts' (digital copies of programmes) or audiobooks, which you can listen to on your computer or a portable 'MP3' player, such as an iPod.

- BBC podcasts:
  www.bbc.co.uk/radio/podcasts/directory
- UK podcasts: *www.ukpodcasts.info*
- Britcaster: *www.britcaster.com*
- iTunes: *www.apple.com/uk/itunes*
- Audible: *www.audible.co.uk.*

Directory enquiries

- Yell: *www.yell.com*
- BT: *www.thephonebook.bt.com*
- Thomson Local: *www.thomsonlocal.com*
- 118 118: *www.118.com.*

Finding tradespeople

- National Builders Federation:
  www.builders.org.uk
- Federation of Master Builders: *www.fmb.org.uk*
- The Institute of Plumbing and Heating Engineering (IPHE): *www.iphe.org.uk*
- Find a Corgi registered member:
  www.trustcorgi.com
- National Inspection Council for Electrical Installation Contracting (NICEIC):
  www.niceic.org.uk
- National Association for Professional Inspectors and Testers (NAPIT): www.napit.org.uk.

Getting about

The internet is also a terrific source of useful information to help you plan journeys via public transport and by car.

Any UK national born on or before 2 September 1929 is entitled to a free standard 32-page ten-year passport from the Identity and Passport Service. Find out more at: *www.ips.gov.uk/passport* or by phoning the 24-hour national call rate helpline on 0300 222 0000.

Bus/train

- Department of Transport information about concessionary bus passes: *www.dft.gov.uk/pgr/regional/buses/concessionary*
- Wales Concessionary Travel: *www.newydd.cymru.gov.uk/topics/olderpeople/transport/*
- Scotland Concessionary Travel: *www.scotland.gov.uk/Topics/Transport/concessionary-fares*
- Northern Ireland Concessionary Fares Scheme: *www.drdni.gov.uk/index/smart60.htm*
- Senior Railcard: *www.senior-railcard.co.uk*
- National Rail: *www.nationalrail.co.uk*
- Transport Direct: *www.transportdirect.info*
- Traveline: *www.traveline.org.uk*
- The Trainline: *www.thetrainline.com*
- Seat 61: *www.seat61.com*
- Transport for London: *www.tfl.gov.uk*
- Eurostar: *www.eurostar.com.*

Maps/routefinders

To help you get from A to B without a detour via X, Y and Z.

- Google maps: *www.maps.google.co.uk*
- Multimap: *www.multimap.com*
- Streetmap: *www.streetmap.co.uk*
- AA Route Finder: *www.theaa.com/travelwatch/ planner_main.jsp*
- RAC Route Finder: *www.route.rac.co.uk.*

Flying

You can track live flight arrivals and departures as well as find useful information about check-in times, baggage restrictions and parking etc. on the website for the relevant airport.

- London Heathrow: *www.heathrowairport.com*
- London Gatwick: *www.gatwickairport.com*
- London Luton: *www.london-luton.co.uk*
- London Stansted: *www.stanstedairport.com*
- Manchester Airport: *www.manchesterairport.co.uk*
- Birmingham International: *www.bhx.co.uk*
- Glasgow International: *www.glasgowairport.com*
- Edinburgh International: *www.edinburghairport.com*
- Belfast International: *www.belfastairport.com.*
- BA: *www.ba.com*
- BMI: *www.flybmi.com*
- Virgin: *www.virgin-atlantic.com*
- easyJet: *www.easyjet.com*
- Ryanair: *www.ryanair.com*
- Flybe: *www.flybe.com*
- Eurostar: *www.eurostar.com.*

Holidays

In addition, the internet can be extremely useful when it comes to planning holidays. You can research destinations and travel options, find hotels and plan activities. You can also book and pay for your holiday online.

Remember to follow the normal guidance about giving your credit card or other personal details to any online company. If you do use a third-party travel agent service, you may wish to check whether your holiday is protected under the ATOL (Air Travel Organisers' Licensing) scheme. Find out more at: *www.atol.org.uk*

- Lastminute: *www.lastminute.com*
- Expedia: *www.expedia.co.uk*
- Opodo: *www.opodo.co.uk*

Find hotel reviews at Tripadviser: *www.tripadviser.com.*

Hobbies

Discover new activities; source supplies and make contact with fellow enthusiasts – all with the click of a mouse.

Education and training

The web is an excellent source of information about opportunities to learn new skills and/or gain qualifications.

IT

- BBC guide to using a computer:
  *www.bbc.co.uk/learning/subjects/
  information_technology.shtml*
- Directgov: Improving your IT skills:
  *www.direct.gov.uk/en/EducationAndLearning/
  AdultLearning/ImprovingYourSkills*
- Learndirect: home/office IT:
  www.learndirect.co.uk
- Learndirect centres across England, Wales and
  Northern Ireland: phone 0800 101 901:
  www.learndirect-skills.co.uk/centres
- Learndirect centres in Scotland have different
  funding: phone 0808 100 1091
- UK online centres: England: phone 0800
  771234: *www.ukonlinecentres.com/consumer*
- Digital Unite: *www.digitalunite.net.*

General

Age Concern Factsheet about leisure and learning:
www.ageconcern.org.uk/AgeConcern/fs30.asp

- Directgov Adult Learning: *www.direct.gov.uk/
  en/EducationAndLearning/AdultLearning*
- Learndirect: *www.learndirect.co.uk*
- University of the Third Age: *www.u3a.org.uk*
- Open University: *www.open.ac.uk*
- Evening classes: *www.hotcourses.com.*

Work

Alternatively, if you wish to find a new career or
set up your own business, you can discover
sources of information, support and advice
online.

- Directgov information about job programmes for over 50s: *www.direct.gov.uk/en/Over50s/Working/LookingForWork*
- Age Positive: *www.agepositive.gov.uk*
- Prime: *www.primeinitiative.org.uk*
- The Age and Employment Network: *www.taen.org.uk*
- Wise Owls: *www.wiseowls.co.uk*
- HMRC guidance for self-employed: *www.hmrc.gov.uk/selfemployed*
- HMRC guidance on setting up a business: *www.hmrc.gov.uk/newbusinesses/tmabeginners-guide-to-setting-up-a-business.shtml*
- Businesslink: www.businesslink.gov.uk.

Family history

There is a wealth of information available online to help you explore the branches of your family tree.

- Government's family record website: *www.familyrecords.gov.uk*
- National Archives: *www.nationalarchives.gov.uk/familyhistory*
- National Archives: Census: *www.nationalarchives.gov.uk/census*
- 1901 Census: *www.1901censusonline.com*
- BBC Family History website: *www.bbc.co.uk/familyhistory.*

Volunteering

If you have some free time, there are lots of sites that can help you find an outlet for your energy.

- Directgov information about volunteering: *www.direct.gov.uk/en/Over50s/HomeAnd*

*Community/Yourcommunityandenvironment/
DG_068414*
- Volunteer England: *www.volunteering.org.uk*
- Volunteer Scotland:
  www.volunteerscotland.org.uk
- Volunteer Wales: *www.volunteering-wales.net*
- Volunteer Northern Ireland:
  www.volunteering-ni.org
- CSV: Retired and Senior Volunteer Programme:
  www.csv-rsvp.org.uk/
- TimeBank UK Volunteering:
  www.timebank.org.uk
- WorldWide Volunteering: *www.wwv.org.uk*
- Reach: *www.reach-online.org.uk*
- Samaritans: *www.samaritans.org*
- Mentoring and Befriending Foundation:
  www.mandbf.org.uk
- The Coaching and Mentoring Network:
  www.coachingnetwork.org.uk.

Summary

These listings are of course not exhaustive, but they do give some idea about the extraordinary range of goods, services and activities you can investigate and do online.

In fact, you may soon find yourself unable to imagine living your previously 'offline' life.

Happy exploring.

10
Glossary

404 Error: An error message you receive when you try to access a web page that either does not exist or is temporarily unavailable.

Anti-virus software: Protects your computer from viruses, malware and spam. Must be updated regularly so is often sold with a subscription that lets you download updates from the internet.

Bandwith: The amount of data that can be carried by your internet connection, usually expressed as kilobytes per second, or kbps.

Bookmark: A way to save internet addresses within your browser so you can easily find them. Bookmarked sites are often referred to as 'favourites'.

Broadband: A permanent high-speed internet connection that is 'always on'. It receives digital information about 100 times faster than a narrow band 'dial-up' connection and does not interfere with the telephone connection. 'Wireless' broadband is increasingly popular, allowing a computer or multiple computers to connect to the internet without the need for wires. It requires a wireless router and can be password-protected to stop others from using your connection.

Browser: A programme that lets you look at or 'browse' websites. Popular browsers include

Internet Explorer from Windows and Firefox from Mozilla.

Byte: Used to measure amounts of computer data. One byte is roughly equivalent to one character (letter, number or punctuation mark) of text. A kilobyte (KB) equals about 1,000 bytes, a megabyte (MB) is around 1,000 KB, while a gigabyte (GB) is approximately 1,000 MB.

CD-ROM: A compact disc storing digital data, such as software, that can be read and processed by your computer.

Cookies: Small files that websites store on your hard drive so they can recognise you when you visit them again and remember your settings or preferences. They are also used to track adverts you have seen. You can set most browsers to reject all cookies, or to ask your permission before storing them, but this can cause problems accessing some sites. It is a good idea to delete cookies after using a public computer, such as in an internet cafe or library.

CPU: Central processing unit. The speed of your processor determines how fast your computer can process data and is usually measured in megahertz (MHz), or gigahertz (GHz).Two of the most popular PC processors are Intel's Pentium and AMD's Athlon.

Dial-up: An internet connection where your computer uses a piece of equipment called a modem to dial a number to gain access to the internet and email etc. Dial-up connections are much slower than broadband, hence they are also called 'narrow band'. You cannot use your telephone to make or receive calls while your computer modem is connected.

Download: A file you have copied to your computer from the internet.

Driver: A piece of software that runs the hardware attached to your computer, such as a modem, printer or scanner. New hardware usually comes with a CD-ROM containing the drivers. You can also download drivers from the internet.

Encryption: A means of encoding data with a secret key or password, making it secure for transmission. Encryption levels commonly associated with wireless networks are 64-bit and 128-bit, with the latter the strongest commercially available.

Firewall: A programme that is designed to block computer viruses or the transfer of unsafe data. Recommended if you have an 'always on' broadband connection.

Hard drive/disk: The part of your computer where you store the operating system, software (programmes) and files such as documents and photos.

Hardware: The physical parts of your computer such as the keyboard, monitor, modem, printer, scanner etc.

History: A list saved within your browser showing the addresses of websites you have visited recently. It is a good idea to delete your history after using a public computer, such as in an internet cafe or library.

HTML (Hypertext Markup Language): The language used to construct web pages.

HTTP (Hypertext Transfer Protocol): The letters at the front of a website address when entered into your browser.

Internet service provider (ISP): A company that provides internet connections. Popular ISPs include AOL, BT.com, Virgin, Tiscali, and TalkTalk.

IP Address: The numerical address of each computer connected to the internet.

Logging on: Accessing the internet.

Logging in: Accessing your account on a particular website after entering security information such as a username, password, PIN code etc.

Logging off: Signing out of your account on a particular website or leaving the internet altogether.

Mac: A type of computer developed by Apple. Macs have a different operating system and different technical specifications to those of personal computers (PCs) and some financial institutions' websites cannot be properly accessed by Macs.

Malware: Software downloaded from the internet and installed onto your computer without your knowledge for malevolent purposes, including displaying unwanted ads (adware), installing more unwelcome software, or spying on your activities (spyware) to capture information like usernames and passwords, which are then sent back to a fraudster who tries to access your online accounts.

Memory: The amount of storage capacity on your computer, including fast temporary storage areas that allow the processor to find the data it needs quickly in order to carry out various tasks. Adding extra memory to your computer can massively increase its speed.

Modem: A piece of hardware that is used to connect computers to the internet. It is provided free with most internet packages.

Operating system: A master programme, which runs automatically when you switch on the computer and which supports all other programmes. The most popular PC operating system is Microsoft Windows, the newest version of which is called Vista.

PC: Originally short for 'personal computer', now the standard name for any non-Mac computer.

PDF (Portable Document Format): A popular format often used for online versions of printed documents such as manuals, application forms and terms and conditions. PDFs cannot be altered, only viewed. You may need to install free software from Adobe Acrobat to be able to read PDFs.

Phishing: A type of internet fraud in which you receive an email purporting to be from your bank or other financial provider. It invites you to 'confirm' your details, but directs you to a fake website where fraudsters hope to capture your confidential personal information. You should never respond to any email that asks you to do this, and never enter your details into a website whose address you did not enter directly or reach from another site you trust.

Rebooting: Restarting your computer, either by shutting it down properly and restarting (a soft reboot) or by switching it off and on again (a hard reboot). Hard reboots are not good for your computer and should only be done as a last resort.

Router: A piece of hardware that connects your computer to the internet. Most broadband packages include a router. A wireless router allows wireless access to the internet.

Search engine: A website that indexes other sites and lets you search its database to find material on particular sites. The most popular search engine is Google.com, but others include Ask.com, Yahoo! and Live.com. Dogpile.com lets you search a number of search engines at the same time.

Software: Computer programs and applications a computer needs to work effectively.

Spam: Commercial emails sent out in bulk mailings. Most ISPs offer spam filters designed to stop such emails from arriving in your inbox.

Trojan: A programme like a virus, which is disguised as a harmless piece of software, such as a game, but which, when launched, actually sabotages the computer on which it is running. Never install software if you do not trust the source.

Upload: A file you have copied to the internet from your computer, e.g. photographs you copy to a website so you can then order prints.

Virus: A programme that has been designed to damage your computer or operating system. Many viruses are now transmitted via email attachments, which is why you should never open an attachment if you do not recognise the sender's address and know what it contains. See **Anti-virus**.

VOIP (Voice Over Internet Protocol): A system that lets you use your computer to make cheap or even free telephone calls over the internet. Popular VOIP providers include Skype and Vonage.

Webmail: Email accessed through a website that can be reached on any computer (such as Hotmail or Yahoo!) instead of through a dedicated email programme installed on the hard drive of your own computer. Many ISPs allow you to access the same email account through both routes although webmail often offers fewer functions.

Index

The four national Age Concerns in the UK have joined together with Help the Aged to form new national charities dedicated to improving the lives of older people.

Age Concern Books

Age Concern Books publishes a wide range of titles that help thousands of people each year. They provide practical, trusted advice on subjects ranging from pensions and planning for retirement, to using a computer and surfing the internet. Whether you are caring for someone with a health problem or want to know more about your rights to healthcare, we have something for everyone.

Ordering is easy To order any of our books or request our free catalogue simply choose one of the following options:

☎ Call us on **0870 44 22 120**

🖱 Visit our website at
www.ageconcern.org.uk/bookshop

✉ Email us at
sales@ageconcernbooks.co.uk

You can also buy our books from all good bookshops.